MANCHESTER DISCOVERED

by

urban**MCR**

CONTENTS

INTRODUCTION 6

CASTLEFIELD 10

Roman Fort   11
Bridgewater Canal   14
Beetham Tower   16
Birdgewater Hall   18
Museum of Science and Industry   19
Castlefield Art Gallery   20

SPINNINGFIELDS 22

People's History Museum   24
John Ryland's Library   25
Opera House   27

CIVIC QUARTER 29

Manchester Town Hall   30
St Peter's Square   32
Central Library   33
Albert Square   34
The Hidden Gem   35
Manchester Art Gallery   37
Albert Hall   39

CENTRAL RETAIL DISTRICT 41

Royal Exchange Theatre   42
Exchange Square   44
St Ann's Church   45
Portico Library and Gallery   47
The Printworks   48
The Arndale   49

MEDIEVAL QUARTER 51

Manchester Cathedral   52
National Football Museum   54
Chetham School of Music and Library   56
Manchester Arena   58

NORTHERN QUARTER 59

Afflecks	61
Band on the Wall	62
Centre for Chinese Contemporary Art	64
Manchester Craft and Design Centre	65
Manchester Police Museum	66

CORRIDOR MANCHESTER 67

Victoria Bath's Trust	68
The Whitworth	71
Elizabeth Gaskell's House	73
Manchester Museum	75

TRAFFORD CENTRE 78

Trafford Centre Attractions	80
Chill Factore	82
Jump Nation	82
Soccerdome	83
Airkix	83
Eventcity	84
Sea Life	84

SPORTSCITY 85

Etihad Stadium	87
Manchester Regional Arena	89
Philips Park	89
Manchester Velodrome	90

THE QUAYS 91

MediaCity UK	92
Old Trafford	93
Imperial War Museum North	95
Emirates Old Trafford	97

INTRODUCTION

Manchester. A city of magnificent history, unique culture and exciting attractions. Located in the heart of North-West England, the centre of the UK's most populous urban area outside London has so much to offer. Experience the amazing diversity of the various areas of the city and immerse yourself in the huge array of entertainment, leisure and tourist hotspots. Delve into the music and media, science and engineering, architecture and sports which make the city so memorable. Whether visiting to conduct business in this global economic city, interested in exploring the best of British culture or simply looking to unwind on a relaxing and enjoyable vacation, Manchester will both meet and exceed your expectations.

The early origins of Manchester date back to the year 79AD, when the fort of Mamucium was built by the Romans and civilisation first established in the local area. This was constructed in between two rivers, the River Medlock and the River Irwell, forming the basis of the modern English county of Lancashire. The name, oddly, is thought to have been a Latinisation of an original Celtic name, literally meaning 'breast-shaped hill'. From there,

the city's modern name evolved, with residen of Manchester now commonly referred to a 'Mancunians'. Further on in this book, a section o Castlefield details the area where the foundation and the Roman fort itself are still visible to this da However, Roman civilisation in the UK ended i the 3rd century, with their withdrawal creatin a vacuum which was filled by the Anglo-Saxon migrants from the Germanic tribes of continenta Europe. This was also about the time whe Scandinavian people gradually settled around th Lancashire and neighbouring Chesire region of England. Following the Norman conquest England in 1066, much of the surrounding are was destroyed by the subjugating of the North William the Conqueror. Over the next few decade and centuries, Manchester would remain a relative small and local township as the North of Englan rebuilt itself from the ruins, struggling to grow du to a lack of proper industry.

The true personality and character of Mancheste became evident from around the 13th to 14t centuries, when there was said to have been massive influx of weavers and textile maker also from the Germanic/Dutch ethnic group of continental Europe. This created Manchester's strong foundation in a tradition and industry of trading wool and linen. Also at around this time, the famous Manchester Cathedral was built in 1421 with the Chetham's School of Music housed within. In the 1600s, the city's fabric production was in full swing, and production gradually switched to cotton as the Industrial Revolution began within the next couple of hundred years.

Manchester was central to the beginnings of the Industrial Revolution which would go on to sweep the nation and then the Western world, became the world's first industrialised city within less than a century. This led to unplanned urbanisation on a massive scale, a huge boom in the population and production and the point at which Manchester started to grow from a township to a fully-fledged city. The famous Bridgewater Canal was originally opened in 1761 with the first modern railway system in the world later opened in 1830, allowing for the transportation of goods on a massive scale into and out of the city. In 1852, the city opened the original buildings of the UK's first public library. Manchester, which had become known as the 'Cottonopolis', then went on to achieve city status a year later, becoming the first new British city for 300 years and paving the way for other previously less populous areas of England to expand and industrialise.

The city's textiles industry declined during the second half of the 19th century as other parts of the world continued to develop their own cotton manufacturing. However, Manchester's industrial status proved crucial through the two World Wars in the first half of the 20th century, as a centre of manufacturing for the war effort. This soon made Manchester a key target for bombing by Nazi Germany's 'Luftwaffe' air force, and the city was extensively blitzed during 1940. The historic city centre was heavily damaged, houses were razed to the ground and the restoration of the seriously damaged Manchester Cathedral took the next two decades to complete.

At around this time period, Manchester also became a global centre of science and engineering. In 1904, salesman Charles Rolls met engineer Henry Royce at The Midland Hotel, marking the start of a great British partnership of the car industry. Furthermore, the Nobel Prize winner Ernest Rutherford is widely credited with having first discovered the nuclear atom, split the atom and thus initiated the entire field of nuclear physics in a Manchester laboratory from 1907-19. And the first programmable computer, the Small-Scale Experimental Machine (SSEM) also known as the 'Baby', was designed and built at The University of Manchester in 1948, taking up most of a large room. These incredible, ground-breaking achievements had their roots in the industrial entrepreneurship

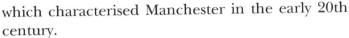

which characterised Manchester in the early 20th century.

The 1950s and 1960s saw the effective closure of heavy industry on a large scale, including cotton production, in Manchester. Changing policy shifted the UK's outlook from manufacturing industries to a largely services-based economy. The Bridgewater Canal was no longer able to handle the much larger container ships which start venturing into its ports, which caused them to close down in 1982. Factors such as these meant that the North of England, including Manchester, suffered greatly from economic loss, with over 150,000 job losses occurring from 1961-83. Despite this gloomy period for the city, a musical counter-culture lead by famous rock groups such as The Sex Pistols, The Smiths and The Stone Roses lead to the formation of the drugs-and-rock-fuelled 'Madchester' music scene in the 1980s, followed by famous British pop groups such as Oasis and Take That in the 1990s.

In contrast with the decline of heavy industry, tourism started to become an important industry in Manchester in the late 20th century. The Museum of Science and Industry opened in 1969 followed by the Museum of Transport ten years later, and in the 1980s Castlefield officially became an Urban Heritage Park with careful reconstruction of

the original Roman fort. In addition to this, the retail scene of the city exploded as the switch to services took place. The original Arndale Centre opened in 1976, with the city's Chinatown being established in the same decade. More recently, the renowned out-of-town Trafford Centre opened in the Greater Manchester area in 1998, followed by the nearby Lowry Art Gallery in 2000. Many more attractions were also built during the same time period, as comprehensively covered in the rest of this book. Ultimately, the de-industrialisation of the city during the 20th century has allowed a large suburban population to form, improved living standards and lead to the development of Manchester's state-of-the-art services towards the end of the second millennium.

The late 1980s also saw the large-scale regeneration of Manchester. Major initiatives were planned and implemented to revitalise the city, such as the 'Metrolink' tram network, the first outside London and still the largest outside London in the UK today. Modern construction of the Bridgewater Hall and the Manchester Arena helped to create a new and more modern image for the city, with former shortfalls becoming catalysts for further evolution. The IRA bombing of the city centre in 1996 and the upcoming 2002 Commonwealth Games mean that much of the city centre was improved and built

afresh, which has further led to a diverse range of modern urban attractions springing up across the city.

Today, the city is particularly famous for its high-profile contributions to both sports and media. Two of the world's most famous and successful football clubs, Manchester United and Manchester City, regularly represent the city in both the UK's renowned Premier League and on a global stage. Manchester has hosted every major domestic and international football competition in which it plays a part, including the 1966 World Cup won by England. The city also has numerous athletes, rugby players, swimmers, cricketers and cyclists who all compete on the highest international levels. As well as this, Manchester is home to many of the BBC's and ITC's most well-known television productions, including Blue Peter, BBC Sport, The Jeremy Kyle Show and the famous Coronation Street. With such a large array of brands rooted in Manchester, it's no wonder that the city has spread its modern reputation around the world.

Manchester is a focused city which continues to grow and expand with the modern era. From a small township to the industrial centre of the world and now a modern metropolis of media, retail and sports, Manchester certainly has evolved through the ages. If you were to visit the city in a few decades time, perhaps it would have evolved into yet another new role on the global stage. But whilst the city continues to develop and diversify, it still retains its oldest and most valuable cultural traditions. Each of the wonderfully diverse stages of Manchester's history have made their mark, meaning the city has become a vibrant and exciting hub for locals and tourists alike. Voted the best UK city to live in as part of the Global Liveability Survey 2015 and beating London for the second year running, Manchester is a real British gem. We hope you enjoy our guide to the exploration of this outstanding city as much as we enjoyed writing it!

CASTLEFIELD

Castlefield is a beautiful historical area of inner-city Manchester which became the United Kingdom's first Urban Heritage Park, designed to preserve the history of the area and influence future planning applications. It is the birthplace of Manchester, the site of a Roman fort called Mancunium, from which the area transformed into Manchester today over many centuries. It is the perfect place for a relaxing walk, offering unparalleled views of the canals.

Alongside the picturesque canals, where the boats and buildings reflect dramatically in the water, numerous bars and restaurants are present and offer incredible food and drink, becoming an increasingly popular destination for visitors of Manchester.

Castlefield has transformed from a neglected corner of Manchester to a major thriving attraction with frequent events that prove popular with both local residents and tourists. A fantastic mix of canals, wharfs, railways and historical sites together with quality local pubs, bars and restaurants means that Castlefield has something for everyone to enjoy.

Roman Fort

In 79AD, General Agricola led his army of Roman soldiers into the North West of England. They decided to select Castlefield as the location for the fort due to its strategic advantages, being built on a rocky outcrop protected by the rivers of Irwell and Medlock. It guarded the road between the Roman settlements of Eboracum and Deva, now known today as York and Chester respectively. Mancunium was the name of the fort in the Roman province of Britannia, from which Manchester was named. It is the very first definite record of a human settlement in Manchester.

The fort was originally built out of timber, with defensive walls made of soil; although this was later enlarged and rebuilt with stone instead in around 200AD, when Emperor Severus came to the North of England to subdue a revolt. The inside of the fort contained the commander's house, granaries, stables and barracks for 480 soldiers - which would later be able to house nearly 1000 people when rebuilt. This Roman fortress would have contained soldiers from every corner of the Roman Empire, with merchants and military units from Spain, Austria and Hungary.

A civilian settlement was established around the fort, but when the Romans left this village in 410AD to defend Rome from the Barbarians, it was eventually abandoned. This area was subsequently used for agricultural purposes. In later years, a new village called Manchester was established a kilometre from the site - the same city we are talking about today. As Manchester expanded during the Industrial Revolution, the construction of the Rochdale Canal, as well as the building of viaducts for the Great Northern Railway, damaged the remains and destroyed much of the fort.

The North Gate and defensive ditches, which remained relatively intact, were restored in 1987 following extensive archaeological excavation by the Greater Manchester Archaeological Unit. The preserved remains of the Mancunium fort can still be seen today, with peaceful green surroundings complementing a relaxing walk through the Roman Fort in Castlefield.

Bridgewater Canal

The Bridgewater Canal is England's first ever man-made canal, and was key to the industrialisation of Manchester. It has a proud heritage dating back to the 17th July 1961, and famously named after the 3rd Duke and 6th Earl of Bridgewater, Francis Egerton. The Bridgewater Canal revolutionised transport in the country, as well as revolutionising Manchester, marking the beginning of a golden canal era which lasted until 1830.

Originally, the Duke transported his coal along the River Mersey and Irwell as well as using horses - however, he soon realised that both of these methods were inefficient and expensive. Francis Egerton's inspiration for this impressive landmark came from European countries such as France and Italy, following a grand European tour that he had embarked on at the time. Evidently impressed with these advanced transportation systems, he successfully made it his personal mission to bring this technology back home to influence canals in Britain. This caused an extreme and intense period of canal-building, which later became known as 'Canal Mania'.

The equivalent cost of building the preliminary stage of the canal from Worsley to Manchester today is an eye watering £23,000,000. However, due to the vast advantages of the canal over transportation by natural rivers or land, the price of coal was cut in half. Furthermore, the Bridgewater Canal was considered to be a significant major engineering achievement, believed to be the greatest such achievement in the United Kingdom by many. Despite many objections from a number of parties about the extension of the canal, it was given royal consent in 1952. This allowed the further construction of the canal from Manchester southwards to go ahead, and the cost of this project soared once more to approximately £30.2 million.

Even at 60 years of age, the Duke took the project further and managed to secure his fifth Canal Act in 1795, linking up Worsley and Leigh and allowing the Leeds to Liverpool Canal to interconnect. Throughout the years, the canal's ownership has changed many times, having been sold by the initial canal trustees to the Bridgewater Navigation Company Ltd in 1872 for £1,120,000. Only 13 years later, however, the canal was sold to the Manchester Ship Canal company for almost £2 million. Today the Bridgewater Canal Company Ltd is responsible

for the care and maintenance of the Bridgewater Canal.

A trip to the Bridgewater Canal is a fantastic day out for people of all ages, with a variety of different activities for everyone to enjoy. The canal is a great place for a tranquil walk or bicycle ride with superb views. There are also peaceful fishing areas on various stretches of the Canal for a relaxing and enjoyable afternoon. Canal boats are available to hire for the day, with plenty of pubs and restaurants situated very close to the waterfront.

Beetham Tower

Beetham Tower is the tallest (and perhaps the most recognisable) building in Manchester, standing at a breathtaking 169m tall (554 feet). With 47 storeys, this landmark is one of the most visible icons in the city. It is home to the five-star Manchester Hilton Hotel, 219 luxury apartments and 16 penthouses. The tallest skyscraper in the city is visible from 10 surrounding English counties on a clear day, and is both the 7th tallest building in England and the tallest outside London. It was completed in 2006 at a staggering cost of £155 million, with a fireworks display held to celebrate the construction of the highest point.

Beetham Tower has featured in many different television programmes including Vertical City and Britain From Above, as well as having been shown in the opening sequence of multiple television series including The Street and Coronation Street. It was designed by the well-known architect Ian Simpson, and is located on a very narrow plot of land. The architect himself went on to purchase the penthouse on the top floor, the highest living space in Britain, costing him £3 million and occupying two storeys.

The famous Beetham Tower 'whistle', which both intrigues and annoys many nearby residents, is an intermittent humming noise which can sometimes be heard in windy weather. The mysterious noise is thought to be caused by winds hitting the glass blade on the top of the building, and has even caused disruption to the production of Coronation Street. Although attempts have been made to solve the issue - including installing foam pads, aluminium nosing and fixing further attachments to the blade - the well-known problem still remains to this day.

With the first 22 levels occupied by the Hilton Hotel, the 23rd floor is home to the world-renowned Cloud 23 Bar, which offers spectacular 360-degree panoramic views across Greater Manchester and beyond. Overlooking the iconic cityscape, these views can be enjoyed whilst tasting some of the best cocktails in the city or an afternoon tea with handmade cakes and warm scones, making it a truly unforgettable experience.

Bridgewater Hall

The Bridgewater Hall is a concert hall which costed about £42 million to build, named after the Third Duke of Bridgewater who commissioned the adjacent canal to be built through Manchester. The hall has housed the renowned Hallé Orchestra since 1858, as well as being regularly hosting the BBC Philharmonic Orchestra, although its current, soundproof structure was officially opened in 1996 by Her Majesty The Queen and the Duke of Edinburgh. The Manchester City Council received funding from the European Regional Development Fund in order to plan and build more recent construction for the hall, which currently boasts seating for over 2,000 across 4 tiers and red sandstone architecture.

The centrepiece of the hall is a magnificent £1.2 million, 5,500 pipe organ which at the time of its construction was the largest instrument built in Britain for over 100 years. The hall also hosts a number of restaurants and bars, including the Charles Hallé restaurant, a favourite amongst concert-goers due to its award-winning cuisine. Sensational concerts and events continue to make the Bridgewater Hall a central part of Manchester musical history, which is a must-visit place for anyone interested by the opportunity to hear performances of the highest calibre.

The hall is constructed on a bed of 280 springs which help to reduce external noise and enhance its excellent acoustics, making the hall the first built using such technology. The building Is built using solid, reinforced concrete with a stainless steel outer shell, further contributing to the noise cancellation and keeping out the urban sounds of the adjacent road and Metrolink line. These expensive yet effective features serve to demonstrate the high quality nature of the hall, built to showcase some of the finest musical concerts and displays from across the world. The Bridgewater Hall consolidates the fine architectural and artistic heritage of Manchester, whilst being a flagship symbol of Manchester's modern regeneration.

Museum of Science and Industry

Also known as MOSI, the Museum of Science and Industry focuses on Manchester's history in a vast array of areas including transport, aircraft, railway, power, textiles, communications and computing. The museum includes the site of Manchester Liverpool Road, the world's first passenger railway station. It first opened in 1969, then called the North Western Museum of Science and Industry, and the council subsequently purchased part of the Liverpool Road station from British Rail in 1978 for a token amount of £1. Since then, the museum has expanded to include the entire former station, symbolic of the rich heritage of Manchester's history.

The museum merged with the National Science Museum in 2012 and is now part of the Science Museum group, a body of the Department for Culture, Media and Sport. Housed in five listed buildings, the museum itself is an architecturally and historically significant part of local heritage. It includes a hands-on science centre, working cotton machinery in a Textiles Gallery and steam mill engines in the Power Hall. Other attractions include an Air and Space Hall dedicated to Manchester's role in the history of flight, as well as a 4D theatre featuring moving seats and blasts of air to bring the historical experience to life.

The Museum of Science and Industry also holds many unique scientific exhibitions, and has hosted an annual science festival since 2007. These exhibitions include part of the world's first commercially available computer, the models used by John Dalton to demonstrate his atomic theory and one of the world's largest collections of working steam mill engines. The museum offers daily practical demonstrations for a taste of history, such as spinning and weaving using original machinery. Providing a fascinating window into Manchester's rich industrial and scientific past, this museum is definitely worth a visit.

Castlefield Art Gallery

Located close to Deansgate Station lies the influential hidden gem that is Castlefield Art Gallery. The ideology behind Castlefield Art Gallery centres around a determination to bring local artists as well as those further afield into the limelight, thus expanding the art scene in the North West. The gallery is mainly home to contemporary visual artists, spread over two floors with a feature wall spanning both floors.

Founded in 1984 by the Manchester Artists Studio Association, the gallery regularly partners with various universities such as the Manchester School of Art (part of Manchester Metropolitan University) and the University of Salford, giving students the opportunity to host 'launch pad' sessions allowing the use of the gallery as a test bed for their work. Today, you can visit a variety of exhibitions with each one lasting for approximately two months each, showcasing the fantastic artwork that Manchester has to offer.

SPINNINGFIELDS

Specially developed in the 2000s, Spinningfields is a business, residential and retail sector in the centre of Manchester, located between Deansgate and the River Irwell. At a staggering £1.5 billion cost, the project consists of 20 buildings covering approximately 430,000 square metres of residential, retail and commercial space. The project was orchestrated by Allied London Properties with the aim of creating a central business district that would be a hub for finance and business at the heart of Manchester.

The area takes its name from a narrow street running westwards from Deansgate, 'Spinningfield'. In 1968, the area was reformulated into Spinningfield Square, before the region was later officially named Spinningfields. The square was born out of the demolition of the old Manchester Magistrates' Court in 2006, forming an area that was never intended to become a public space. However, such was the potential for the area in the concrete-heavy centre of Manchester that Allied London soon thought best to make it as reclusive area of luscious

greenery, peeping out of a surrounding concrete and crystal jungle.

The 2007-2010 financial crisis caused the development of Spinningfields to falter somewhat. Fortunately, this was only a temporary deviation from its fast-paced growth, as Manchester City Council agreed to buy freeholds worth roughly £15 million in the region soon after. Allied London's marketing of the development as the 'Knightsbridge of the North', having letted shops in Spinningfields The Avenue to Emporio Armani and other similar high-end shops, came under intense scrutiny due to its abysmal performance, with Manchester Evening News describing the area's flagship thoroughfare as a 'ghost town'. This was in stark contrast with the thriving bohemian Northern Quarter, situated just a stone's throw away.

However, despite Spinningfields' initial poor performance in retail, the area has gone from strength-to-strength in more recent years, dominated by commercial office developments and

even being likened to London's thriving Canary Wharf by the Financial Times. Anchor tenants include Barclays, Deloitte and HSBC, as well as numerous impressive buildings located on The Avenue. Residential buildings such as the 16-story Leftbank Apartments overlook the River Irwell, with picturesque views across the whole of Manchester, especially on days when it isn't raining. Admittedly, these can be few and far between!

Spinningfields is also home to the enthralling People's History Museum, as well as various courts of law including the adjacent Manchester Crown Court and the impressive Civil Justice Centre. This is an 80 metre tall building completed in 2007, and is the first major court complex constructed since the Royal Courts of Justice were completed in London in 1882. There is also an integral social aspect to this broadly commercial area; for example, the open-air cinema in the centre of Spinningfields. This creation of this cinema is a feat which has gained regional recognition, with Spinningfields being voted by Manchester residents as being the most family-friendly area in Manchester in 2013 in a survey by the hotel chain Premier Inn.

Whether to experience the spectacular high-rise buildings, indulge in one of the upper echelon restaurants or merely soak up the vibrant atmosphere; Spinningfields is definitely an excellent place to go, even if just to walk through. If you do decide to walk through the area, you may just find yourself becoming inadvertently drawn in by the wonderful attractions that Spinningfields has to offer!

The People's History Museum encapsulates the democratic nature of Great Britain, providing an apt portrayal of the lifestyle of ordinary British people over the past 200 years. Detailed information on fundamental issues and staple topics ingrained in British culture is displayed at the museum, such as the Women Suffrage Movement, Popular Radicalism and football, presented in the form of galleries and regularly updated exhibitions.

A £12.3 million development with overwhelming views of the meandering River Irwell, the museum is a splendid portrayal of the natural human instinct to strive for social justice. Originally situated at Lime House Town Hall, it was later moved to Manchester in 1990, with a gallery being introduced in 1994. In 2001, the buildings became known as the People's History Museum after an attractive glass walkway was constructed to link the two buildings.

The museum is home to one of the largest collections of political memorabilia in Britain, including over 2,000 posters, 300 political cartoons, 7,000 trade union badges and tokens and over 95,000 photographs. In addition to this, with over 400 trade union banners in their collection, the People's History Museum boasts the world's largest such collection, a riveting portrayal of the means British society has used to strive for equality.

John Rylands' Library

A stunning neo-Gothic style sandstone building, the construction of John Rylands Library began in 1890, and following ten years of lengthy construction work it opened on January 1st 1900. Rylands' wife Enriqueta wanted to build the Library as a tribute to her late husband. Having been impressed with Basil Champneys' design of Mansfield College, Oxford, she commissioned the architect to design the library, which subsequently became widely regarded as his most outstanding achievement. Enriqueta used the £2.7 million John had left her from his cotton trading empire (equivalent to a staggering £240 million today) to construct a building enriched by sheer architectural beauty.

Champneys' rose pink, Cumbrian sandstone design ensured that the library turned out to be what many would consider the finest in Britain. The central feature of this phenomenal feat of architecture was its ground-breaking use of electricity, making it one of the first buildings in Manchester to be lit by Manchester, with its electricity generated near the building until mains electricity was introduced in the 1950s.

The revolutionary nature of the building, which emulated the ethos of John Rylands himself, was further typified by the fact that it bore one of the world's first air-filtration systems in order to reduce air pollution inside the building. Enriquetta was the epitome of perfectionism and is said to have fretted, often arguing with Champneys and Cassidy, over the very slightest details on the marble statues of herself and her husband that flanked the historic reading room, such as their shoe sizes and her late husband's beard.

The library is home to undisputedly one of the most impressive collections in Britain, with thousands of manuscripts from all over the world and from many different periods of history. These include manuscripts that cover all major European and Middle Eastern dialects, constituting a magnificent overall collection written in over 50 languages. These artefacts are from a time period spanning the last five millennia and are written on a vast variety of mediums, such as bamboo, copper, ivory, papyrus and vellum.

More specifically, the collection includes the earliest known fragment of the New Testament from the 2nd Century, the oldest piece of Western printing from 1423, and an incredibly rare example of the misprinted 'wicked' edition of the Bible. As well as these exceptionally rare relics, the library is also home to an abundance of archives concerning both local businesses and well-known religious institutions.

In 1972, The John Rylands' Library merged with The Manchester University Library following a sustained period of financial struggle which had massively restricted the Library's self-sufficiency. As well as ensuring the library stayed open, this merge also led to the introduction of some collections from the Joule Library, previously part of the University of Manchester, to the John Rylands' collection. This has further expanded the works held in the library. Such a historic collection is considered highly valuable by many experts, and so great care is taken to ensure it is kept safe for future generations to come.

Opera House

THE · PLAY · MIRRORS · LIFE

DIRECT FROM THE LONDON PALLADIUM ⚫ ⚫ LET THE MEMORY LIVE AGAIN

Designed by the architectural firm of Farquharson, Richardson and Gill, the Manchester Opera House gained instant recognition as an 'elegant' building by the 'Builder' magazine - a justified description of its architectural beauty. Opening on Boxing Day of 1912, it was initially known as 'The New Theatre', with 'early door' tickets on sale for the sensational production of Kismet. These widely coveted early door tickets enabled the audience to enter the theatre an hour early to shelter from the unpredictable Mancunian weather, as well as helping to avoid the problem of overcrowding.

The theatre's inaugural three years were unfortunately turbulent, with the theatre struggling against renowned competitors such as the Palace Theatre. In 1915, it was sold and underwent rebranding including renaming the theatre to 'The New Queen's Theatre'. Within the next five years, the theatre exhibited countless riveting performances including mesmerizing works from Sir Thomas Beecham and his orchestra; in honour of this illustrious man, the theatre was renamed 'The Opera House'.

The Second World War - in particular, the Manchester Blitz in 1940 - was a period which inflicted terrible destruction throughout Manchester resulting in the obliteration of 165 warehouses, 150 offices, 5 banks and over 200 businesses within a mile radius of the renowned theatre. Miraculously, the Opera House escaped relatively unscathed, a feat which ensured that the theatre's development and evolution towards establishing itself as one of Manchester's most notable theatres did not falter. This stroke of luck meant that the Opera House was considered Manchester's pre-eminent theatre up to and around the 1960s.

However, the Opera House was forced to close soon after for three fundamental reasons. Firstly, television began to take over, lowering the demand for theatre tickets; secondly, the number of theatre competitors within the area was increasing; and finally, the cost of putting on shows was rising. The fateful decline of the Opera House, a theatre steeped in history, continued up until 1979, when it reopened as a bingo hall for the following 5 years.

However, in a dramatic change of fortunes, the Opera House was sold to the Palace Theatre Trust in 1984, who had previously refurbished Manchester's Palace Theatre in splendid fashion. The trust went on to resurrect the Opera House as a theatre and it was reopened in spectacular fashion, with Princess Anne an attendee of the royal opening gala. Since then, the Opera House has been subjected to countless takeovers, yet has continued to flourish as one of the greatest theatres in Manchester.

Incessantly staging various magical shows, the theatre has been embedded in the enjoyable memories of the thousands who have had the pleasure of witnessing them. Such shows have included Andrew Lloyd Webber's The Phantom of the Opera, Barnum, Oliver and a myriad of others. A night at the Opera House promises to be a memorable one, with several spine-tingling musicals, dazzling concerts and entertaining pantomimes every year. A performance at the iconic Opera House is undoubtedly worth experiencing, especially if you've never visited before.

CIVIC QUARTER

The Civic Quarter is arguably the most iconic area in Manchester, home to spectacular listed buildings such as the Town Hall and Central Library. As the beating heart of the Industrial Revolution in the late 19th century, Manchester grew at a phenomenal rate. Invention and innovation were combined with enterprise and a strong sense of honour, pride and citizenship. These were the qualities reflected within the architecture and the public spaces. The Town Hall Complex and Albert Hall represented civic pride and governance, whilst the Central Library provided education that was accessible for all.

Over the past few decades, the extensive regeneration of the area has led to the Civic Quarter leading the way in regards to Manchester's economic growth. It is a fantastic area to visit, with architectural and engineering achievements that can be witnessed and which Manchester can be proud of.

Manchester Town Hall

Manchester Town Hall sits proudly in Albert Hall as an iconic landmark of Manchester. It is rightfully considered as one of the greatest and finest Gothic buildings in the United Kingdom. The designer of such a spectacular building was Alfred Waterhouse, who successfully managed to overcome 137 talented architects to win the competition to design the town hall. The key to Alfred Waterhouse's design – who later went on to design the Natural History Museum in London – was his unique yet ambitious triangular design, which optimised the use of an asymmetrical, oddly shaped plot facing Albert Square.

This eccentric approach allowed the town hall to be as large and magnificent as possible, which matched the council's objective of creating a building "equal if not superior to any similar building in the country". This was achieved at a gigantic cost, believed to be around £1 million, which in today's money is a staggering £80 million. It took 9 years and 14 million bricks to finally complete this historic landmark.

However, when the construction had been completed, Queen Victoria refused to attend the opening ceremony. Instead, Abel Heywood, the mayor at the time, officially opened the Town Hall on 13th September 1877, and it was proposed that there would be a procession of trade societies involving the working people to add to the ceremony. 69 trade societies took part, with an estimated 50,000 people in attendance in a procession that stretched over a mile and which took almost three hours to complete. Each society donated an item of their trade as a symbol of how great Manchester was, with a 16 pound loaf donated by the Union of Operative Bakers!

Weighing 8 tonnes, with 23 bells, Great Abel – the famous clock bell named after Abel Heywood - is an astonishing 87 meters tall, which is one of the tallest buildings in Manchester, ringing for the first time on New Year's Day 1879. Great Abel can be heard throughout Manchester, and was essential to workers to tell them the time in the Victorian era. The exquisite level of detail is evident throughout the whole structure of the building. There are golden cotton buds on top of Great Abel to symbolise the proud fact that Manchester was the international centre of cotton trade. Despite looking comparatively small, each single golden cotton bud is over 6 feet tall.

With over 314 rooms around the central space, there are many architectural and minute details that are incredibly impressive once they are noticed, yet despite the detail the Town Hall is spacious and well balanced. There are statues commemorating the people that have been important to Manchester, including Agricola in the grand entrance, St George on the gable, Henry III and Elizabeth I. The grand ceremonial hall features a series of 12 murals by Ford Madox Brown that picture the key moments in Manchester's history.

The Manchester Town Hall is a popular attraction for both locals and tourists alike, available to marvel at no cost. The Sculpture Hall café also provides a location to immerse yourself within the city's rich history, with a range of hot and cold drinks and meals available, with a North West inspired menu of breakfast, lunch or afternoon tea. Clock Tower tours are also available, providing spectacular views from Great Abel, as well as guided Town Hall tours. The Manchester Town Hall is a place you simply have to visit.

St Peter's Square

St Peter's Square is home to the Manchester Cenotaph, a memorial made out of Portland stone by Sir Edwin Lutyens in 1924 to remember those who lost their lives in the First World War. It features a Peace Garden as part of the memorial, and is also the location of One St Peter's Square and numerous high-rise office blocks built as part of the £20 million regeneration scheme. The square was the site of the Peterloo Massacre in 1819, then known as St Peter's Field. Throughout England, but especially prevalent in Manchester, the divide between the rich and poor was increasing, resulting in periods of famine and unemployment. The poor economic situation enhanced the appeal of political radicalism. On 16th August, the Manchester Patriotic Union, a group desperate for political reform, organised a demonstration led by the radical orator Henry Hunt.

A large crowd of around 70,000 gathered, some of whom were families on a day out in the summer. The local magistrates panicked due to the large numbers, ordering the military authorities to arrest Hunt and disperse the crowd. The cavalry charged into the innocent crowd with swords drawn and in the ensuing tragedy, 18 people are estimated to have been killed, and over 700 men, women and children sustained extremely serious injuries, despite the assembly being peaceful, conducting themselves with dignity and discipline.

A journalist by the name of John Edwards Taylor who was able to escape spent two days travelling to London, and managed to get the story published nationally. The country was shell-shocked and the national papers shared the horror of the story. The Peterloo Massacre was one of the defining moments of its age, a view shared by historian Robert Poole. It caused the government to crack down immediately on reform. In reaction to what he had seen, John Edwards Taylor went on to establish the Manchester Guardian newspaper. As a direct result, the massacre also led to the Chartist Movement, which led to the establishment of trade unions. Peterloo was hugely influential in ordinary people winning the right to vote, giving us the democracy we enjoy today.

Central Library

The Central Library is the second-largest public lending library in Britain, with a staggering 35 miles of shelving holding up to a million books. In 1850, Manchester was the first local authority in Britain to provide public lending of books, and a free library was first opened in 1852 in a ceremony attended by Charles Dickens. Since then, the library has moved a number of times to various places in Manchester including a wing of the Manchester Royal Infirmary and an old hut, until its current dedicated building was finally opened in 1934 by King George V. With striking circular architecture composed of a large round base with 2nd-century Corinthian pillars, the library is a magnificent piece of Manchester's history.

An extensive selection of historic books, including 30 books written prior to 1500 and many first editions of major works, includes Shakespeare's Second Folio and a handwritten copy of a Roman codex from the 12th century. Extensive records on the theatrical history of Manchester, as well as works by the famous Mancunian writer Elizabeth Gaskell, are just a few of the collections available at the library. The library also offers multiple computers and four floors of literature. Regular users of the library in the past have included writer Anthony Burgess and Morrisey, the lead singer of The Smiths.

The library underwent modern renovation from 2010-2014, and now much more of the building is directly accessible to the public. It targets young readers much more, even including a 'gaming area' with games consoles, alongside a specially designed children's library modelled on The Secret Garden, famously written by a local writer. The entrance has been restored in great detail, with a glass mural depicting some of Shakespeare's most loved characters, as well as a dedicated 300-seater reading room on the first floor of the building. In essence, the Central Library combines the old with the new, a vast array of Manchester's historical works of literature and stunning classical architecture complemented by a modern and spacious interior.

Albert Square

Albert Square is a public square in front of Manchester Town Hall, containing a number of monuments and statues. The largest of these is the Albert Memorial, a dedication to Prince Albert from Saxe-Coburg, Germany, consort of Queen Victoria, who the square was named after. Prince Albert was well-loved, especially in Manchester - whereas Queen Victoria was thought to have disliked Manchester, Prince Albert was known for his appreciation of the city. When he died suddenly at a young age of 42 in 1861, it plunged Queen Victoria into a deep mourning that lasted the rest of her life.

Manchester Corporation's Monuments Committee decided to erect a memorial to Prince Albert, receiving much public support, including the donation of 50,000 bricks towards the construction by the Bricklayers' Protection Society, ''as an expression of sympathy towards our belove Queen''. The Grade I listed commemoratic features a marble statue of Albert, with the desig personally approved by Queen Victoria.

Each gable within the canopies represented symbolic figure or art or science including Rapha and Shakespeare. Manchester's Albert Memori was the first of several throughout the countr including a similar memorial in Kensingto Gardens, London, completed several years aft Manchester's monument. Within the square the are several other monuments including Bisho James Fraser, John Bright, Oliver Heywood, an William Ewart Gladstone. There is also a founta which was designed by Thomas Worthington, th same designer as the Albert Memorial, to mark th Diamond Jubilee of Queen Victoria in 1897.

The Hidden Gem

St Mary's Roman Catholic Church, which is more often known as The Hidden Gem, is the oldest catholic church in Manchester, built in 1794 to serve the poorest of the city's population, intentionally positioned in one of the worst of areas of Manchester at the time. Hidden away in the corner of Mulberry Street, The Hidden Gem is aptly named due to its difficulty to find.

In 1833, Father Henry Gillow made the decision to re-roof the church and redecorate it with the help of the congregation without any expert builders to oversee the project, which eventually led to the collapse of the roof two years later, severely damaging the structure of the church. Although suggestions were made to find a new site for the church, the unfortunate timing of the outbreak of plague (the Manchester typhus epidemic of 1837) lead to the death of Father Gillow and made this task almost impossible.

St Mary's Church was rebuilt on its existing site by architect Matthew Elison Hadfield. In 1869 Father John Newton took charge of the church, enlisting a

sculptor to design and implement all of the carving that is showcased in the interior of the church today. Figures of Angels can be found on top of the marble high altar, and life size figures of Our Lady and many saints are present, carved with incredible attention to detail, which are stunning to look at even by the standards of today. The Adams Station of the Cross can also be seen within the church, now considered to be one of the great art commissions of the 20th Century.

spectacular tall buildings of the new commercial centre. Despite the many changes that have taken place over the years, the feeling of ''wonderful amazement and ... utter peace'' remains. The free daily access to the church is appreciated by both Catholics and non-Catholics alike. The beautiful church of St Mary's remains the favourite attraction in Manchester for many visitors, and is a stunning place which is definitely worth visiting.

Manchester Art Gallery

Located at the heart of the city and one of Manchester's oldest and most stunning cultural institutions, Manchester Art Gallery is a glowing representation of Manchester's esteemed culture. The gallery is a publicly owned establishment, open seven days a week and attracting more than half a million people each year, with free admission a further bonus. This allows people from all backgrounds to lavish in the enlightening pieces on display.

Despite not being open in 2002 following fundamental renovation works (totalling a remarkable £35 million), the main gallery was built for an academic society in 1823, where the building was originally called 'The Royal Manchester Institution for the Promotion of Literature, Science and the Arts'. Today, the gallery extends across three connected buildings, two of which are listed and designed by the nationally acclaimed architect Sir Charles Barry.

Home to a range of works by both local and international artists, the Gallery's stunning collection spans over six centuries, with some of the exceptional collections dating back to the 1400s. Among the gallery's admirable collection are over 200 oil paintings, 3000 watercolours and drawings, 250 sculptures, 90 miniatures and around 100 prints. Furthermore, the Gallery's remarkable collection consists of over 13,000 various objects, widely ranging from ceramics to doll houses and metalwork, and illustrating the compelling art on display. Perhaps most notably, the oldest artefact possessed by the gallery is an ancient Egyptian canopic jar, circa 1100 BC.

Several works by the prominent French impressionist

Pierre Adolphe Valette, a teacher in Manchester in the early 20th century, are also on display. His works include surreal portrayals of the foggy Mancunian streets and canals. However, the Gallery's collection of Victorian art is perhaps the largest, most notably that of the Pre-Raphaelite Brotherhood and Victorian Decorative Arts. Works on show from this period include Ford Madox Brown's iconic 'Work' and Millais's breathtaking 'Autumn Leaves.'

With the introduction of a new exhibition every couple of months, the Art Gallery is ever-changing and there is always something new to see. In order to gain rich cultural knowledge from your visit, there are numerous tour guides available to be booked, offering a phenomenal knowledge of the gallery. Situated on Mosely Street in the City Centre, it is easily accessible via public transport, with the Metrolink stops 'Piccadilly Gardens' and 'St Peter Square' a mere 2-minute walk away. Likewise, if you are planning on travelling by bus, the nearest stops are 'Piccadilly Gardens' or those on Princess Street, only a short distance away.

Albert Hall

Originally built as a Methodist Central Hall in 1910, the Albert Hall of Peter Street, Manchester is a splendid, Grade II listed Wesleyan chapel that is currently a prominent venue for music concerts. Prior to renovation in 2012-13, the Chapel Hall had been unused since 1969, untouched and hidden from Manchester for over forty years. The resurrection of the Albert Hall was orchestrated by 'Trof', a venue behind 'Gorilla' and 'The Deaf Institute', two famous bars in the centre of Manchester. A building enriched by architectural splendour and artistry has been furnished with a modern, state-of-the-art and purpose-built music hall. This is undoubtedly one of the most atmospheric music and events venues in the UK.

Throughout the year, there are countless live music and club events and as the venue continues to increase in popularity and receive wider attention, it attracts the very best acts. As a result, it has played host to Sam Smith, as well as many other leading artists in the music industry. With external Gothic and Baroque features, the Albert Hall's interior includes a horseshoe gallery, sloping floor and coloured roof lights, capturing the venue's party atmosphere. Easily accessible by train and tram, with Deansgate train station in close proximity as well as the St. Peter's Square Metrolink a short walk away, it is well worth a visit, especially for those who want to experience an enjoyable night out in Manchester.

CENTRAL RETAIL DISTRICT

Home to a large number of shops, restaurants and tourist attractions, the Central Retail District is famous for what it has to offer. The extremely popular Manchester Arndale is situated in the midst of Market Street, Deansgate, King Street and Victoria train station, among other renowned locations.

In addition to this, the Manchester Arena plays hosts to major musical events on a regular basis, as the biggest indoor arena in the UK. The Printworks, a vast entertainment centre including the largest cinema in the Manchester city centre and many bars, restaurants and nightclubs is a vibrant and enjoyable centre of Manchester's nightlife.

Major attractions aside, the Central Retail District hosts a huge number of shops, making it the biggest city centre shopping mall in the UK. With practically every high street name having a presence, as well as many more upmarket stores, the district is a shopper's delight. Record visitor numbers and spending attract many millions of visitors to the area

annually, making it a hub for businesses and retail in Manchester. Excellent transport links also make the district a central part of visiting Manchester, with links to all other major areas of the city.

The 1996 IRA terrorist bombing has also led to redevelopment on a vast scale within both the Medieval Quarter and this district. The bombing caused widespread damage to the infrastructure and economy of Manchester city centre, requiring a large amount of investment to repair the damages and revitalise the area. The world's biggest branch of Marks and Spencer was built in the area, with Selfridges co-occupying the building and the Arndale Centre being reconstructed as a brand new development. This redevelopment has placed the area among the top retail centres in the UK. Right in the heart of Manchester, the Central Retail District is potentially the most popular area for tourists in Manchester, as one of the most modern and exciting parts of the city for anyone to visit.

Royal Exchange Theatre

The Royal Exchange is one of Britain's most loved and most distinctive theatres. Built in 1809, it was originally used to trade yarn during the cotton boom, in which Manchester was a pioneering city. A staggering 80% of the world's cotton was traded in Manchester, earning its title Cottonopolis, and it was traded in the Royal Exchange. The colossal Great Hall was once considered the biggest room in the world. With over 16,000 members, the chaotic cotton trading spilled out into the street. It was the world's centre for cotton trade, until the building was bombed during the Manchester blitz of the Second World War.

However, when the cotton trade began to decline due to foreign competition in 1968, the building was under the threat of being demolished. After remaining empty for 5 years until 1973, it was taken over by a theatre company. Subsequently, the Royal Exchange Theatre Company was officially founded in 1976 with the largest arena theatre space in the whole of Great Britain, and is now the longest serving group theatre in the country. Unfortunately, the blitz of the Second World War was not the last time that bombing damage was inflicted upon the building.

In 1996, an IRA bomb was detonated less than fifty meters from the building, inflicting devastating damage, although the main structure itself remained undamaged. It took two years, a massive £32 million funded by the National Lottery and a lot of fundraising to repair the theatre, with performances taking place in an indoor market building at Castlefield in the meantime. Prince Edward officially opened the rebuilt and refurbished Royal Exchange Theatre in November 1998, with production of Stanley Houghton's Hindle Wakes.

the same play that had been running when the bomb went off.

The unique design of the Royal Exchange Theatre never ceases to amaze visitors on their first visit. It is a seven-sided, steel and glass-walled capsule that is literally suspended from huge marble pillars in the Great Hall. This unusual yet brilliant design is intended to create a close relationship and welcoming atmosphere between the actors and audience, with every seat in the theatre less than nine metres from the circular stage. The stage is surrounded on all sides by seating. This 750-seat theatre remains the only theatre in the world which is suspended from above, designed partly due to the fact that the floor of the exchange was unable to take the 150 tonne weight of the theatre and the audience.

Even today, you can visit the Royal Exchange building, look up and be able to see the original trading board with the final day's trading closing figures. Experiencing a theatre show at the Royal Exchange is unforgettable with a rich spectrum of shows on offer, presenting the best that world theatre has to offer from classical productions to modern repertoires.

Exchange Square

On Father's Day on 15th June 1996, the biggest bomb ever to hit mainland Europe was set off by the IRA and exploded in central Manchester, completely wiping out Corporation Street in Manchester City Centre. The tragedy left 212 people injured and tore through several buildings, completely demolishing them and leaving £700 million worth of widespread damage - more than £1 billion today. A prior tip-off meant that miraculously, there were no deaths, as most people were evacuated safely. After the bombing, the local community refused to be divided by the chaos and worked together to rebuild the city square, leading to a complete regeneration of the area.

Following the calamity, the rebuilding and rebranding of this section of the city was completed just in time for the millennium at a cost of £1.2 billion. One such rebranding included Exchange Square, which was built to relocate damaged shops such as Marks and Spencer's, with the whole project led by architect Ian Simpson. Today, a post-box which miraculously remained standing and virtually undamaged, marks a spot just a few metres from where the bomb exploded.

Now, Exchange Square is known to be one of the major shopping areas in the centre and is home to the new Cathedral Street, housing major worldwide fashion brands such as Louis Vuitton, Hugo Boss, Ted Baker, Burberry and many more. Alongside this array, the square also includes a branch of Selfridges, the Corn Exchange and an entrance to the famous Arndale Centre.

St Ann's Church

St Ann's Church is a particularly significant building as its tower marks the exact point of the centre of Manchester. It was built on a large cornfield named Acres Field at the beginning of the 18th century, as Manchester was growing from a small village to a small rural town. It was the second church to be built in Manchester after what is now Manchester Cathedral, and was much needed due to the growth of the city. The rather expensive funds were provided by Lady Ann Bland, whose patron saint the church is named after as a tribute. St Ann's was consecrated in July 1972.

The church was built as an impressive building, with the neo-classical design all constructed from a locally quarried red Collyhurst sandstone. As the stone was naturally very soft, some of the original stone has since been replaced with sandstone of various colours, sourced from the counties of Lancashire, Staffordshire, Derbyshire and Cheshire. The interior of the church was intentionally plain as the reformation was taking place in England, having become a Protestant Christian country under the rule of King Henry VIII. Protestants in the Tudor times believed that churches should be plain to allow people to concentrate on the sermons.

In 1887, the interior was redesigned by Alfred Waterhouse, the famous architect of the Town Hall. Many things were adjusted and changed, including the layout and location of the stairs and gallery at the West End. He also installed stained glass windows and created the Lady Chapel, which contains the painting 'The Descent from the Cross' brought from Italy by a churchwarden of St Peter's. St Ann's narrowly escaped the damage done during the Manchester air raids in World War II - it still has a burnt out incendiary bomb which fell onto the roof of the church.

Decades later in 1996, St Ann's Church was just as lucky when the IRA bombing devastated the city centre. Although the windows were blown out, there was no structural damage, which meant no rebuilding was required. This was because the Royal Exchange Theatre adjacent to St Ann's took most of the damage, shielding the small church from any significant harm. It was also fortunate that the organ was preserved, as it had by chance been taken out for refurbishment when the bombing took place.

After more than 300 years of existence, the historical church still continues to host frequent music concerts and recitals, with regular performances by students from the Royal Northern College of Music. St Ann's Church remains a peaceful place of worship, and with enjoyable events taking place regularly it is a fantastic place to visit.

Portico Library and Gallery

A self-governing subscription library, the Portico Library and Gallery was built from 1802-1806 in the emulative, classical architectural style of the 'Greek Revival' movement. Iconic sandstone columns and steps at the front of the library are brought together by a traditional rectangular plan and a neo-classical interior. The library itself was initially also created with the purpose of being a 'newsroom', where the upper class gathered to quite literally read the news shipped in from across the globe. As times moved on and such news became widely available to the masses, a beautiful glass-domed ceiling was inserted at gallery level in about 1920 as the building became more open to the public.

This prestigious library has since partnered with numerous other local and national institutions, including the People's History Museum, in the spirit of nurturing the arts on a wider-reaching level. It has exhibited both established and new artistic talent since the 1960s, including works by famous author and illustrator Beatrix Potter, and the gallery area was formally opened in 1987

in order to build upon the success of these past exhibitions. Having had many famous members in the past such as Sir Robert Peel and John Dalton, the library is a successful example of the way in which Manchester's rich culture has brought works of writing and art together.

The main proportion of the library is a collection of 19th century literature, an exclusive area with access restricted only to members and researchers. It provides an insight into Victorian culture and history, with a wide range of original works, detailed novels and biographies available. However, the gallery area, exhibitions and events are open to the general public, with modern construction enabling disabled access. The Portico Library also offers a series of prestigious literature prizes, such as the Portico Prize for Literature established in 1985 to recognise works of poetry, fiction and non-fiction set in the North of England, as well as a more recent award launched in 2015 to celebrate young writers of the North West.

The Printworks

Constructed in 1873, the building was originally called the Grove Printing House and was owned by the wealthy 19th century newspaper proprietor Edward Hulton. As its initial name suggests, the building's primary function was the printing of newspapers. Following the takeover of the premises by the Allied Newspapers consortium in 1924 (renamed Kemsley Newspapers in 1943), it became one of the most prolific printing houses in Europe, responsible for the printing of massively influential newspapers such as the Sunday Times and the Daily Mirror. In 1959 it was rebranded Thomson House, following the purchasing of Kemsley Newspapers by the Canadian businessman Roy Thomson. The site housed a printing press until 1985, when it was retired due to a high-profile pensions scandal.

After lying dormant and disused for several years after its closure, the IRA bombing in 1996 served as a catalyst for inner city rejuvenation. In 1998, the derelict building and the adjoining site were purchased by Shudehill Developments for the sum of £10 million. In reference to its former printing heritage, the building was subsequently named The Printworks. A £110 million restoration and conversion project was then set in motion by the new owners, aiming to completely transform the property into one of Manchester's most engaging entertainment venues. Although the interior was utterly transformed, the project planners took great care in ensuring that the impressive stone exterior and the core architecture was retained. Finally, on the 9th November 2000, the Printworks was officially opened by guest celebrities Sir Alex Ferguson and Lionel Ritchie.

Following The Printworks' extensive transformation, the 365,000-square-foot facility is now set over four floors with diverse facilities that include a 20-screen Odeon cinema complex with North West England's first IMAX screen, a Virgin Active fitness club, a Hard Rock Café restaurant and a 'Tiger Tiger' nightclub, as well as many more. The central location makes it an ideal place to visit and spend a few hours of the day, with the rest of Manchester quite literally minutes away. With just about every form of entertainment one could possibly want, The Printworks is a Manchester attraction for all to enjoy.

The Arndale

The Manchester Arndale is Europe's largest city-centre shopping complex and is situated on Market Street in Manchester city centre. With 41 million annual visits, the centre boasts a branch of practically every well-known department store and retail outlet imaginable. The Arndale property trust was first acquired in 1968, just prior to a public enquiry into the redevelopment of Market Street at the time. The construction of the original buildings took place in stages and was finished in 1979, taking 7 years to build a total of 210 shops and 200 market stalls at a £100 million cost. As a result, by the 1980s the centre of Manchester had become a vibrant retail area, rejuvenated from its previous industrial and commercial state.

However, the original centre, while hosting a number of malls and famous stores such as Littlewoods and BHS, was criticised for its architecture. The exterior was considered a somewhat ugly example of modern architecture, and was covered by pre-cast concrete panels faced with brownish and yellowish ceramic tiles. In 1996, the IRA bombing of Manchester city centre dealt significant structural damage to large parts of the centre, requiring the demolition of certain stores including Marks and Spencer and proving extremely costly. This led to required redevelopment on a huge scale, which was subsequently undertaken over the following few years. As part of the renovation, the majority of the previous exterior tiles were removed and replaced with a sandstone and glass exterior.

The Next store at the Arndale Centre is the company's largest, as well as having the largest glass front in the UK. The new architecture and expansion of the centre have allowed for a much more modern complex, accommodating even more major retailers than before. A Harvey Nichols store, Selfridges and The Printworks can all be found within a few minutes walk of each other. In addition, a 20-screen Odeon cinema and over 15 bars, clubs and restaurants provide high quality entertainment and places to eat out for shoppers and tourists. The Arndale Tower, the 5th tallest building in Manchester, hosts dedicated office space, and the entire complex has its own 1,450 space multi-storey car park. Manchester Arndale is an excellent example of the changing face of Manchester, with roots in its industrial history while also offering one of the most modern and stylish retail experiences of the city.

MEDIEVAL QUARTER

A truly historic area of the city, the Medieval Quarter (also known as the Cathedral Quarter) consists of buildings and architecture which have stood for hundreds of years. Contrasting with the more modern face of Manchester, the quarter includes the famous 600-year-old Manchester Cathedral, Chetham School of Music, Chetham's Library and the National Football Museum among its attractions, just to name a few. The area is divided from Salford by the River Irwell, which runs directly between the two cities, with the magnificent fountains of Greengate Square situated right next to this natural border.

As part of the redevelopment after the 1996 IRA bombing of Manchester city centre, the outskirts of the Medieval Quarter received a few new additions. Exchange Square, home to New Cathedral Street on which Harvey Nichols and Selfridges stores are located, provides a more modern feel to this classic area. An entrance to the Manchester Arndale at the edge of the square, one of the most-visited shopping centres in the UK and the main attraction of the neighbouring Retail District, can be accessed. This redevelopment has effectively helped to revive and modernise the area, meaning that tourists visiting the quarter can experience both Manchester's rich cultural history and its modern shopping attractions.

The area has numerous high quality pubs and restaurants to complement its historic buildings. Two historic pubs, the Old Wellington Inn and Sinclair's Oyster bar, are situated between the cathedral and the Corn Exchange. The former dates back to the 1550s, and both pubs were moved brick-by-brick to their current location after the IRA bombing, remaining highly popular to this day. Numerous restaurants offering a high quality range of international cuisine are also situated in the area, making the quarter a 'food destination' for many visitors. The modern aspects to the quarter are complemented by many tourist attractions, providing a warm flavour of urban Manchester for those visiting the historic site.

Manchester Cathedral

Manchester Cathedral is one of only fifteen Grade I listed buildings in Manchester, measuring over 220 feet long and 82 feet wide. It boasts the widest nave (central congregation area) in the country. Manchester Cathedral has been present in the city's history for the majority of 1000 years. The present church was built in 1215 by Greslet, Lord of the Manor and 5th Baron of Manchester, who decided to build a church adjacent to his Manor house. The Greslet family coat of arms is still used by the church today.

However, it wasn't until 1421 that Thomas de la Warre (who became a Baron in 1398) was granted a license from both King Henry V and Pope Martin V to establish a collegiate church in Manchester. The parish church became a Collegiate Foundation, and was dedicated to St Mary, St Denys (patron saint of France) and St George, perhaps reflecting Henry V's claim to the French throne.

At the time the cathedral was being built, the peop of England were still very religiously devout, wit strong belief that heaven, hell and purgatory Catholic term for where the cleansing of souls tak place before entering heaven) existed. Relativ on earth would pray for the soul of their loved on in the hope of quicker passage from purgato into heaven. Hugely impressive, highly decorate chantry chapels were also built, memoria dedicated to the memory of a person or a famil with money offerings known as 'indulgences' als donated to the church.

The Gothic styling of the magnificent buildin reflected these views, with the spires pointin directly upwards to heaven. However, when Kin Henry VIII split with Rome in 1534, England becam a Protestant Christian country without a belief i purgatory. Henry's son Edward VI was strong

Protestant, and ordered the chantry chapels to be taken down.

Now the parish of the Bishop of Manchester, the Cathedral attracts many visitors due to its delicate carvings and fine stained glass windows. The choir stalls have a 'misericord' (ledged) seating arrangement, and are described as being some of the finest in Europe. Many carvings of medieval tales and legends illustrating moral messages can be found on the underside of these seats. The Healing Window, a stained glass tribute installed in 2004 to commemorate the restoration of the cathedral following the 1996 IRA bombing of the city centre, gains particular interest. As one of the most interesting churches in the land in the heart of Manchester, the cathedral is most definitely a special place to visit.

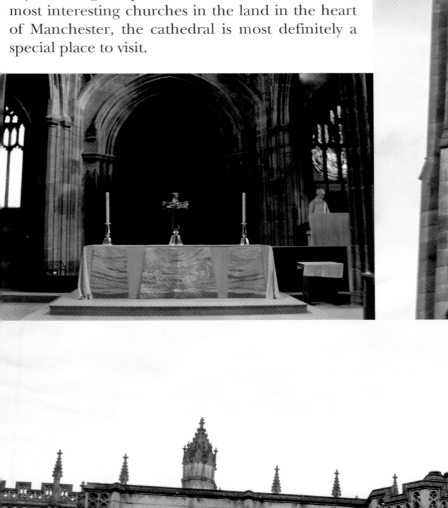

National Football Museum

Preston North End, a founding member of the Football League and competitor in the Football League's inaugural season's home ground (the historic 'Deepdale') was the National Football Museum's original home in Lancashire, Northern England. Opened in 2001 following a significant grant from the Heritage Lottery Fund of £7.5 million to fund the project, the National Football Museum's overall cost escalated to £12 million. Ironically, it was funding that was the museum's fundamental issue, with £790,000 income against £1,230,000 outgoings in 2007 ultimately leading to evasive action by the trustees, negotiating a £2 million per year offer for a move to Manchester.

The museum's negotiators were Manchester City Council, who facilitated investment from the European Regional Development fund and reopened the museum at Urbis in July 2012, a mere two years following its unfortunate closure in Preston. Designed to the exact specifications of Manchester architect Ian Simpson, the stunning six-story glass building is simply a marvel of architecture. With its unique, sloped structure, Urbis' quintessential design ensures it is an iconic image of Manchester - an apt location for the splendour of the National Football Museum.

Preceding opening, trustees initially targeted 350,000 visitors per year. However, following a blisteringly encouraging start (with 100,000 visitors in the first six weeks), the objective was obliterated a few months before the initial goal, at the end of April 2013. The museum's popularity didn't seem to falter in the slightest, with over 1 million registered visitors in just over two years. However this mesmerising success came as no surprise with visitors from all four corners of the world enticed by the phenomenal array of footballing memorabilia on display. There are over 2,500 footballing artefacts displayed at any one time and over 6,000 altogether. Accompanied by state-of-the-art interactive displays and a vast selection of exhibitions, the National Football Museum truly offers something for everyone.

The remarkable collections are arguably the museum's principal attraction and are collated from a rich variety of sources, the earliest of which being the 'FIFA' collection assembled over thirt

years ago by the 'football-crazy, football-mad' Harry Langton, a London journalist who adored 'the beautiful game'. This particular collection consists of the early history of football throughout the world complemented by a stunning football art collection and football paraphernalia accumulated throughout history. Another of the most notable collections at the museum is the 'UEFA Library Collection', held and updated on behalf of UEFA. This collection boasts over 8500 items including reports, brochures, posters and DVDs all related to the European Championships and the history of UEFA.

If you are not that enthralled by historical information, the unique array of interactive activities offers an exciting museum experience. Step into Joe Hart's shoes as you test your reaction times as a goalkeeper; step into the boots of Xavi and Iniesta in the 'tiki-taka' passing accuracy game; can you handle the insurmountable pressure of stepping up to take a penalty against the computerised goalkeeper? And find out if you have what it takes to be the next Howard Webb as you try your hand at refereeing. These interactive activities are aimed at implementing an educational facet in tandem with having fun, with details on performance and the means top athletes use to overcome the stresses and strains of being an elite athlete. Such details may even be used to support the next generation of Cristiano Ronaldos and Alex Morgans in reaching the very top of the game.

The magnitude of the museum, a memento for football over the years both nationally and internationally, justifies the transcendent names on the list of ambassadors for the museum. The President of the museum is the esteemed Sir Bobby Charlton (Manchester United and England legend), with Vice Presidents including Sir Alex Ferguson (arguably the best manager of all time) and Sir Geoff Hurst, scorer of a famous hat-trick in the 1966 World Cup Final accompanied by the classic words 'They think it's all over… it is now!' as the third goal went in at Wembley. The museum's 'Special Ambassador' is Mark Lawrenson, iconic former Liverpool defender, perhaps now best known for his role as pundit on Match of the Day.

Chetham School of Music & Library

Chetham's is a school steeped in history, dating back to the early 14th century, where the land was acquired by the de la Warre family. Naturally, as the school's origins date back 600 years - in which time Britain has incredibly been under the rule of the House of Lancaster, House of York, the Tudors, the Stuarts, The House of Hanovarians and the Windsors - an exact construction date is not known. However, it is thought to have been constructed between 1424 and 1429, taking an extraordinary thirty years to complete. Considering the architectural splendour of the buildings, this comes as little surprise as it is one of the largest buildings in Manchester.

Having served as a church for almost a century, Chetham's was dissolved under the English Reformation in 1547. Elizabeth I re-established it as 'Christ's College' in 1578 until Manchester Cathedral was formed in 1847. During this period, the civil war forced the college to be used as a prison whilst under the ownership of Lord James Stanley,

until Parliament confiscated the land following h execution in 1651.

Richard Dutton was established as the fir headmaster of the college in 1655 and extensi repairs to the college were completed in 165 the year in which the first official students we registered. 9 years later, the college became a incorporated charity. Boys were admitted to th institution based on their predicament and thus th charity could alleviate their needs. The 1870s wa a record decade for the college, with attendanc higher than ever, for the first time exceedin the admittance of 100 people. 1878 served as th year architect Alfred Waterhouse designed a ne schoolroom, synonymous with the Tudor style c building which was popular 300 years earlier.

The abhorrent war years led to arduous implicatio for the school, with attendance falling dramatical to 75 students immediately prior to the First Worl

War. In 1916, at the heart of the War, admittance to the college ceased altogether. Attendance entered further decline two years later with a mere 70 students, resulting from a lack of funding.

The incessant, prolonged bombing of Manchester in the Battle of Britain of World War Two resulted in Chetham's closing down altogether, with resident boys evacuated to Cleveley's in Lancashire, sharing accommodation with a local primary school. The 'Christmas Blitz' of December 1940 led to widespread damage to the building, with the roof burnt by a wrath of fire and windows shattered. This led to a post-war rebuilding phase. Controversially, partially to do with the severe war damage evident on the buildings (or what was left of them) in 1944, local governors campaigned to abandon the site as an institution and proposed it as a religious education site. However, after years of discussion, the school was returned to Manchester.

Recently, Chetham's has been an independent co-educational music school, an arrangement that has been implemented since 1969. Now boasting more than 290 students aged 8-18, Chetham's enjoys the privilege of being the largest specialist music school in the UK and the only specialist music school in the North of England.

Manchester Arena

The 'Phones 4 U' arena is the largest capacity indoor arena in Europe. With a staggering amount of space for over 21,000 people, it is Manchester's premier venue for hosting the greatest events in the music, entertainment and sports calendars. The Manchester Arena has been host to concerts by the music industry's finest, with world-renowned artists such as Lady Gaga and Madonna performing for full-capacity crowds. Despite this, the arena not only hosts world-renowned celebrities, as more regional acts such as Take That and Oasis have also been allowed to perform there. This began even when they were still upcoming stars in order to give them an initial boost that ultimately aided their propulsion to the pinnacle of the music industry, keeping in sync with Manchester's rich music heritage.

Aside from music, the arena hosts some of the most colossal sporting fixtures in the world. Being owned and operated by the highly reputable SMG Europe has proven highly advantageous for the Manchester Arena, as the operations and ground staff employed by the organisation are of the utmost quality - without whom these world-renowned events would not be of the same pedigree. These upper echelon sporting fixtures include countless international boxing championship fights, a vast range of Commonwealth Games events and, perhaps most notably, the 2008 FINA World Swimming Championships. These events are a glowing example of the versatility of the venue that has set it apart as one of the most supreme indoor venues in the world.

Home to over 130 events each year, rarely does a week pass by when the arena has not played host to a remarkable performance or show. This has been recognised internationally, with the arena having won the International Venue of the Year Award in 2001, beating a whole host of other sensational venues around the world.

NORTHERN QUARTER

By the 1840s, the Northern Quarter had become the centre of one of the most important economic shifts in history, with the Industrial Revolution having caused rapid advancement which lead to Manchester claiming the title of capital of the world's textile industry. The development of Smithfield Market and the continued expansion of the cotton industry helped to encourage the Northern Quarter into the industrialisation of the 20th century. Middleton describes an area buzzing with hawkers and processions. However, the cotton trade - the industry that industrial Manchester so relied on - reached its peak in 1912, when 8 billion square yards (6,700 km') of fabric were manufactured and sold from Manchester.

Following the First World War, the high cost of British cotton and the increase in production elsewhere in the world led to a slow decline of the British cotton industry. In the 1960s and 1970s, mills were estimated to be closing at a rate of almost

one per week throughout Manchester and the rest of Lancashire, and by the 1980s only specialised textile production remained. This unsurprisingly had a huge negative impact upon this once thriving area.

In the 1970s, the viability of the Northern Quarter as a commercial hub suffered further from the construction of the nearby Arndale shopping centre, which was completed at the turn of the decade in 1979. Local government was hopeful that the centre, which was one of Europe's largest at the time of its construction, would help to rejuvenate the Quarter's struggling retailers. In fact, it instead compounded these problems to some extent, diverting shoppers away from the smaller, independent shops of the Northern Quarter. The area became characterised by deserted shops and warehouses, and by 1980 almost 25% of tenants had left the once thriving Oldham Street.

The year 1993, however, marked a significant change in the Northern Quarter's fortunes. Following an official study of the area's heritage and character directed by Manchester City Council, the attention of commercial developers became fixed upon the area. The disused warehouses were converted into innovative living spaces, helping satisfy demand for inner-city living, a trend which characterised the early 2000s. Other smaller spaces were also transformed into retail spaces, often by locals, giving the area a unique aura of individuality. Today, Manchester's Northern Quarter is the self-styled creative hub of the city. During its Victorian past, the Northern Quarter used to be an unsafe destination once darkness fell.

Now, it is one of the city's most celebrated areas for nightlife with a wide selection of independent bars and eateries. So, if exploring Manchester's diverse after hours' scene is an activity that interests you, the Northern Quarter is an ideal destination. Equally, during the day the area offers a multitude of different activities. Characterised by its independent stores, the Northern Quarter is perfect for shopping, with fashion and arts being its specialities. A pleasurable day can be had exploring its winding redbrick alleys and industrial architecture. A visit to Manchester just wouldn't seem right without a trip to its famous Northern Quarter.

Afflecks

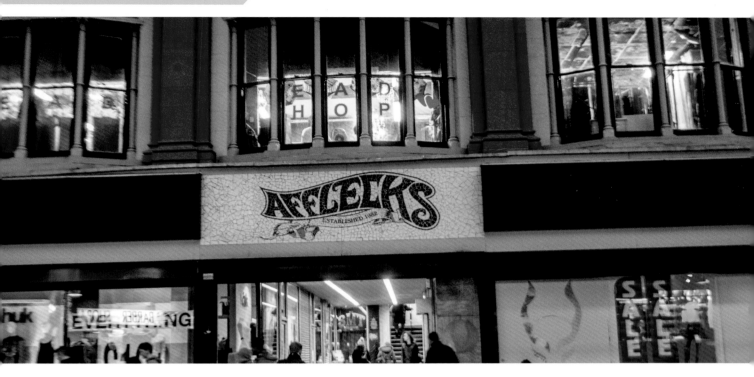

Affleck's was originally founded in 1860s under the name 'Affleck's and Brown', initially existing as a drapery business on Oldham Street. Its rapidly expanding popularity led to it becoming a formal department store, occupying a whole block of buildings between Oldham, Church and Tib Streets. Following an unsuccessful takeover by the department store Debenhams in the 1950s, the decision was made to close Affleck and Brown in 1973.

The doors of Affleck's Palace, the title by which the building is known today, were first opened to the public in 1981 by James and Elaine Walsh. The initial objective of the pair was to provide a suitable environment for aspiring entrepreneurs with affordable rent and no long-term contracts; unit holders operated under a license agreement which allowed them to pay for space on a week-by-week basis. The eclectic atmosphere and maze-like layout of the building led to Affleck's becoming Manchester's primary centre for alternative culture.

Affleck's continued to thrive throughout the 1990s and the locally coined "Madchester Summer of Love", the golden age of Manchester's music scene. As a result of the popularity of iconic Mancunian bands such as Stone Roses, Inspiral Carpets and The Happy Mondays, Affleck's place became the place to go for the latest fashion and musical trends. The markets became characterised by small shops

selling the latest oversized flared jeans and dyed T-shirts alongside numerous record shops. 'Eastern Bloc' was a particularly popular record shop as it dealt in all the latest underground dance tunes of the time.

Once this 'golden age' had passed, Affleck's Palace went through harder times; on March 31st 2008, the market officially stopped trading. However, owing to its position as one of Manchester's cultural institutions, it was bought by Mancunian property developer Bruntwood, who were quoted as saying "Never in our 30 year history have we bought one of our customers' businesses but Affleck's is a Manchester icon that we wanted to protect."

Today, this 5-floor indie emporium is near overflowing with independent sellers, whose wares range from records and vintage clothes to jewellery and artwork. Featuring a café as well as a luxury cereal eatery, there is hardly a more diverse place that can be found in Northern England. It offers a fascinating glimpse into Manchester's underground culture. Indeed, it has been dubbed the North's equivalent of the London's famed Camden Markets. The market's popularity has increased dramatically since the lapse in 2008, and many would say that it is nearing its previous '90s-glory-days' level. All this makes Affleck's Palace is a must-see for anyone visiting Manchester.

Band on the Wall

The story of Band on the Wall dates back to the early 19th century, when a keen publican Elizabeth Marsh opened the doors of her second public house 'George and Dragon'. The pub itself is located at the intersection of Swan Street and Oak Street. In 1803, the year in which the pub originally opened, Manchester was fast becoming the global centre of the rapidly advancing Industrial Revolution and one of the cotton capitals of the world. Swan Street was the working heart of the city where workers worked, lived and socialised, thus placing George and Dragon at the centre of attention. George and Dragon was a place that, despite being around for decades, constantly adapted to reflect the ever-changing culture of Manchester.

The late 19th century sparked different styles of music that were being popularised due to the influx of migrants. Musicians were unable to perform in the street due to strict law enforcement by the Greater Manchester Police, and offenders were liable to be fined 40 shillings. This coincidentally

became a catalyst for the pub music scene, as thes would-be street performers began using pubs as th outlets through which to showcase their talent. B 1892, 512 pubs in Manchester held licenses to allo musical entertainment. As a result of the volume c music-based entertainment occurring at the venue during the 1930s the name of the pub unofficial changed from 'George and Dragon' to the nam it is known by at present: 'Band on the Wall'. Th idea of the name was actually popularised by one c the regular performing musicians at the pub, Erni Tyson.

However, as Manchester's textile industr steadily declined around the mid-20th century many workers became unemployed and wer consequently forced to relocate. The popularit of George and Dragon mirrored this decline. A the 1970s progressed, many local buildings wer demolished and the historic pub suffered greatl Live music became an irregular occurrence. But i 1975, Steve Morris, a local jazz musician, becam one of the owners of Band on the Wall, with plans to convert the long suffering pub into a haven for jazz music. He had a clear vision and an eye for talent; under new ownership, the focus was almost solely on the music.

With the new music programme, the pub became a prime venue for renowned artists at the time including the likes of the Bee Gees, Village People and David Bowie as well as all the latest jazz artists. This rejuvenation happened at a time when the introduction of a new programme called the Manchester Musicians Collective was emerging. This paved a path for new acts such as Joy Division, and a provided a proving ground for more established acts such as the Sex Pistols and the Clash.

Today, Band on the Wall remains a central component of the Manchester music scene, holding regular events and live performances. It is now a non-profit organisation, the principal aim of which is the promotion of some of the UK's best music. The venue prides itself on the diversity of the performers it accommodates, as well as on its local education programme. For those interested in music and popular culture, this historical former pub is definitely worth a visit.

Centre for Chinese Contemporary Art

The Centre for Chinese Contemporary Art, formerly known as the Chinese Arts Centre, is the UK's leading organisation for the promotion of the ever changing international dynamic that is contemporary Chinese art. The organisation was founded in 1986 when Hong Kong artist Amy Lai organised Chinese View '86, the Manchester's first Chinese festival, with the intention of providing opportunities for the Chinese artistic community and developing the positive identity of Chinese culture in Britain.

Initially based in Chinatown, the Chinese Centre for Contemporary Arts was originally a government-funded registered charity. The first large-scale exhibition to be held at the centre was Beyond the Chinese Takeaway in 1992, curated by Kwong Lee and Wendy Hee (then the Director of the Chinese Arts Centre). In 2003, following a £2.5 million Lottery grant donated with the objective of constructing of a flagship centre for contemporary Chinese art, the brand new, purpose-built centre was unveiled. Designed by OMI Architects, the centre won a RIBA prize for architecture and features distinctive wrought iron detailing and a stunning glass atrium.

Today, the centre is based in the Northern Quarter of Manchester, with the renewed focus of making Chinese art and culture accessible to Manchester arts audiences, as well as avoiding association with outdated and overly traditional representations of Chinese culture and folklore. The move across to the Northern Quarter from Chinatown can be seen as a symbol of the cultural shift in the way that the British Chinese community was perceived during this period, and its more complete integration into UK society.

Alongside a regularly changing programme of new exhibitions, the centre also commissions new work and runs artist-in-residency schemes. Furthermore, the centre contains a small visitor shop selling contemporary craft, jewellery and printed materials. Generally known for its lively and innovative programme of exhibitions, residencies, engagement projects, festivals and events, there's always something of note happening at the Manchester Centre for Chinese Contemporary Art.

Manchester Craft & Design Centre

The building in which the Manchester Craft and Design Centre is now located was constructed in 1873 and functioned as a retail fish market. However, in 1973, the market closed down and was subsequently converted into a Craft Village by Manchester City Council, with its public unveiling happening in 1982. Originally operating as an artists' cooperative, it became a not-for-profit limited company in 2003.

Today, the centre's intention is to provide a unique marketplace for the public to browse and purchase an expansive selection of arts and crafts products straight from talented designers. These products include ceramics, bespoke bags, paintings, homeware, and jewellery, among others. The two floor centre holds 18 unique studios containing such items. However, the centre is more diverse than simply offering crafts; there is an on-site café and diverse events occur regularly. The vast array of events held within the centre range from small craft fairs to international showcase events, thus helping local designers as well as displaying pieces from world-famous craftsmen for the public's enjoyment. The aforementioned transformation of the centre was undertaken with care, with many of the original period features still on view. The centre is therefore also of particular interest to those passionate about architecture. Whether you're looking for unique gifts for loved ones or simply enjoy browsing through art, Manchester Design and Crafts Centre is certainly an enjoyable feature of the Northern Quarter.

Manchester Police Museum

Founded in 1981, the Manchester Police Museum was formerly one of Manchester's first police stations, and since has been thoughtfully restored. A particular effort has been made to preserve the building's authenticity, to reflect the reality of policing in the late 1800s/early 1900s. Visitors are able to discover where Manchester's criminals were charged, fingerprinted and detained. There is also the opportunity to admire the grand décor of the Magistrates Courtroom and experience how inmates would have felt standing in the dock, truly bringing history back to life. This immersive experience is particularly popular with children, who often find it exciting to relive the lives of Manchester's best policemen and women. The museum also doubles as an archive, which is available to the public but must be booked prior to making a visit.

A particularly interesting story contained within the museum is that of Jerome Caminada, Manchester's most famous detective and the supposed inspiration behind the world-famous novel Sherlock Holmes. The son of Italian immigrants, Caminada was born in Manchester in 1844. Having grown up among the slums of Deansgate and its crime-ridden streets, he observed first-hand how crime negatively impacts communities.

Later on in life, he used his personal knowledge of the criminal underworld to his advantage as part of his fight against crime in Victorian-era Manchester. Caminada had a very unconventional policing style, which often involved wearing disguises in order to infiltrate criminal groups and gather evidence on suspects. His methods were, in spite of their unorthodox nature, outstandingly effective and helped him to achieve his unparalleled success in catching criminals. Caminada's crime-solving work in 19th century Manchester earned him a place in Manchester's history as the city's first Detective Superintendent.

Now run by ex-police officers and volunteers, the museum is a great way for the general public to understand more about how the city is being kept safe today, as well as to learn about the force's past crime-fighting projects. The Manchester Police Museum is perfect for a family afternoon out, as well as for anyone with an interest in social history in general.

CORRIDOR MANCHESTER

Corridor Manchester is the name formally given to the 243-hectare area of the city stretching from St Peter's Square to Whitworth Park along Oxford Road. The Corridor is the academic heart of Manchester, with the University of Manchester, the Manchester Metropolitan University and the Central Manchester University Hospitals NHS Foundation Trust being situated here. In addition to this, with the next 10 years seeing further planned investment of £1.5billion in the area's major institutions, its growth and significance is sure to continue well into the future. The area's cultural institutions have also been subject to extensive investments projects in recent years, with destinations such as the Whitworth Art Gallery and HOME adding a new dimension to the already vast array of attractions the Corridor has to offer.

Victoria Baths Trust

In 1897, faced with a rapidly expanding population, plans were formed by the Baths and Wash-houses Committee of Manchester Corporation to construct and provide baths to multiple communities residing in and around central Manchester. This was a period during which many people, barring a select few, lacked access to the luxury of warm water or electricity within their homes. Originally designed by Mr Henry Price (the First City Architect of Manchester in 1902), the project was completed by 1906 at a cost of £59,000, a substantial amount for that time.

Despite costing nearly twice as much as other similar facilities, Victoria Baths certainly warranted this higher expense. Hailed by many as the 'Water Palace', the baths were equipped with then state-of-the-art filtration systems and Galloway boilers. Not only was it the pinnacle of functionality, its beautifully decorated interiors proved popular with locals, aptly reflecting the trends of the Edwardian

era. Its facilities notably included Turkish bat[ ] which consisted of 3 different rooms; a 'douch[ ] (shower), 'Russian bath' (steam room) and a re[ ] room.

Aside from the stylish décor, Victoria Baths al[ ] reflected the segregation by class and gender th[ ] was prevalent in the society at that time. Use[ ] found themselves divided into 3 categories: Mal[ ] 1st Class, Males 2nd Class and Females. The cla[ ] in which you were deemed to belong determine[ ] which of the pools you were able to enter. The[ ] imposed restrictions were later gradually reduce[ ] reflecting social progression. After the beginni[ ] of the First World War in 1914, mixed baths we[ ] cautiously introduced, and families were able [ ] swim together for the first time soon after. Ov[ ] time, the activities held by Victoria Baths becam[ ] increasingly diverse. In the 1950s, bowls becam[ ] a popular activity, using the Males 1st Class/Ga[ ] pool whilst it was covered over in the winter month[ ]

with the Males 2nd Class pool later converted into a sports hall.

After approximately 87 years of service, the Manchester City Council decided it was time Victoria Baths was retired, as they could no longer justify the expenditure. The closure was finally completed on 13th March 1993, despite vehement opposition by local residents who clearly still valued the baths. The campaign to restore the baths lead to formation of the Victoria Baths Trust which, as a charity, was able to restore the building whilst preserving all of the Turkish baths and keeping one swimming pool in use. For six years following its closure, the baths stood neglected and as a result, the building declined rapidly. However, the newly formed Victoria Baths Trust was determined to save the building.

In 2001 Manchester City Council granted the trust formal management responsibility of Victoria Baths. This was a move that helped the Baths significantly, as new enthusiasm for resurrecting the once grand building spread. And in September 2003, the Baths won the first series of the BBC's Restoration programme. The building was chosen by a public phone-vote from a short-list of ten buildings in danger of dereliction in the UK, and was subsequently awarded £3.4 million from the Heritage Lottery Fund. The Prince of Wales visited the baths a month later to help celebrate the win. This sparked the full restoration process that restored the baths' former glory. The first phase of renovation work was completed in 2008.

Now restored, Victorian Baths currently plays host to a multitude of events and activities. These include Gin festivals, Vintage fairs and numerous theatrical performances. One ongoing project is the promotion of the arts program in order to establish the baths as a true arts venue for new, contemporary art styles. By doing so, Victoria Baths has become

the perfect place for artists to experiment and showcase new works made available for the public to view and enjoy.

The educational opportunities the centre now offers are also a key feature of the modern Victoria Baths. The baths provide a great setting for children to develop their skills in subjects such as history and art, which are both closely linked to the centre. The building structure and original craftsmanship inside provide inspiration for young artists, as well as giving historians a glimpse of what life was like back in the 19th and 20th centuries. Visitors are able to participate in complete tours of the Victoria Baths, helping to understand the magnificent story behind the building in its entirety.

The restoration has been carried out to an extremely high standard, allowing visitors to truly appreciate the architecture and design just as it was when the baths first opened in 1906. For those interested in history and heritage as well as arts and architecture, Victoria Baths is a wonderful place offering a rich display of culture.

The Whitworth

In 1889, after the Industrial Revolution during which Manchester had been a global manufacturing force, the then-titled Whitworth Institute and Park first opened. The institute was founded by Robert Dukinfield Darbishire, supported by a donation from the famous industrialist Sir Joseph Whitworth. Upon his death, Whitworth bequeathed a sizeable sum of money for the establishment of such an institute, which was to include a technical school, a technical museum, a school of art and an art gallery. In many ways, its foundation was spurred by the city's new-found international status and as a result of this, it was only fitting that it consisted of a variety of museums and other cultural attractions.

From the outset, the Whitworth aimed to bring joy to those from all walks of life through the medium of art. The institute's first purpose-built gallery was opened in 1908, by which time it had already amassed a considerable collection of world-class artwork and textiles. In 1958, the Whitworth became a part of the University of Manchester. Following this merger, the gallery underwent a period of renovation in 1967, helping to transform the Edwardian building's interior into the more modern, open indoor spaces that characterise it to this day.

As a result of its ever-increasing popularity and growing collection, in 2013, the Whitworth experienced its most recent phase of revamping, a £15 million project aimed at further modernising and restoring the building. Two of the most impressive additions were the construction of the new glass-and-brick wings of the gallery, which offer an abundance of natural light and bring an airy feel to the gallery space. The gallery now boasts 55,000 pieces of art and counting. As well as artwork, the centre includes the Clore Learning Studio, a dedicated children's area for messy, creative play.

Following the grand reopening in February 2015,

the Whitworth has played host to several major exhibitions by world-renowned artists. These include the Chinese artist Cai Guo-Qiang, whose exhibition 'Unmanned Nature' featured the draping of an oval room in immense sheets of paper, mottled with markings caused by the sprinkling and igniting of gunpowder on their surface. The Chinese artist used this unorthodox technique to create a breath-taking, serene mountain landscape.

The whole installation was reflected by a pool of water strategically placed in the centre of the room. This exhibition is just one spectacular example of many held at the gallery throughout the year. Whether you're an art connoisseur or are just looking for a fun-filled family outing, the Whitworth is a destination not to be missed.

Elizabeth Gaskell's House

Elizabeth Gaskell was born Elizabeth Stevenson in Chelsea, London on 29th September 1810. Following the death of her mother, Gaskell moved to Knutsford in Cheshire, the town she would later immortalise in her novel "Cranford", to live with her aunt. However, it was later on in her life, after she married her husband William Gaskell in 1932, that she decided to make the industrial centre of Manchester her permanent residence. Gaskell was heavily influenced by her Mancunian surroundings and would often use her literature to highlight the plight of the workers and the poverty that they lived in.

From 1850-1865, Elizabeth Gaskell lived at 84 Plymouth Grove, with the construction of the house itself finished in 1941. During this period she penned nearly all of her famous novels, including Cranford, Ruth, North and South, and Wives and Daughters. She also wrote the biography of her friend Charlotte Brontë, and many fascinating letters. Her husband, William Gaskell, also used the house to hold welfare committees and to tutor the poor. It was the novels written at 84 Plymouth Grove that now cause many to see Elizabeth Gaskell as one of the century's most important female writers. The neo-classical architectural style of the house is now rare in Manchester, as most other buildings from the same time period have since been knocked down due to various reasons. However, unlike the other buildings, 84 Plymouth Grove did not face the same fate, as it was granted listed building status due to its association with the Gaskells, protecting it from demolition.

Following an extensive £2.5 million restoration funded by the Heritage Lottery Fund which helped restore the house to its former glory, it now acts as a fully functioning museum. As part of the renovation, conscious efforts were made so that, once finished, the house would be as authentic and similar to the original as possible. Modern day visitors are able to tour the house, where they will find the house complete with interactive displays, original artefacts, authentic furnishing and décor, as well as a garden consisting of plants mentioned in Gaskell's writing. For those with an interest in Victorian culture and design as well as in classic literature, this attraction is a must-see.

ELIZABETH CLEGHORN
GASKELL
(1810-1865)

Novelist and authoress of 'Mary Barton',
'Cranford'and many other works
lived here
(1850-1865)

118

Elizabeth
Gaskell's House

Open Wednesdays, Thursdays, Sundays 11-4.30
(last admission 4pm)

Admission: £4.95 (£3.95 concessions) for a 12 month
ticket, children under 16 free

Manchester Museum

The Manchester Museum was originally founded in 1821 following the death of John Leigh Philips, a prominent Manchester textile manufacturer with a passion for artwork and natural history. His private collection, which included illustrations produced by the likes of the famously reclusive John Abbot, were to form the basis of the museum's initial collection. From 1835, the collection was then stored on Peter Street. In the 30 years following the museum's foundation, the building began to amass a considerable amount of objects thanks to generous donations from both members of the museum's original society and external donors. A particularly significant addition took place in 1850, when the collections of the Manchester Geological Society were integrated with that of the museum. This absorption added further diversity to the museum's collection.

In 1868, due to a lack of funding and storage for the ever-growing collection, it was transferred to Owens College, which later became the University of Manchester. The new building was publicly unveiled in 1890, with renowned architect Alfred Waterhouse its principal designer. His previous projects had included Manchester's Town Hall and the Natural History Museum in London. Officially named the Manchester Museum, the building came to be used by people of all backgrounds and ages, both for leisure and educational purposes. Not only was the now immense collection often viewed by the public, but schoolchildren were also taught there. A particular example of such an occurrence was during the First World War, a time when schools were converted into makeshift hospitals for those injured on the frontline. As a result, the museum was used to hold classes to the displaced schoolchildren.

Throughout the early 20th century and as a result of the museum's constant expansion, new buildings had to be built alongside the original, which were subsequently opened in 1913 and then 1927. As the collection expanded, so did the staff team that managed it, with the number of employees increasing dramatically. The majority of these were world-class academics, and as a result, the museum became a centre of pioneering research in the natural sciences and humanities. As the museum's collection reached 6 million items, for the benefit of all users, the collection was organised into many different areas including archaeology, botany, zoology and many more. The collection was not the only thing aspect which was increasing, however.

The popularity of the Manchester Museum became a magnet for visitors. Headline exhibitions such as the 'Moon Rock' in 1969 and 'Lindow Man' in both 1987 and 1991 helped to attract up to 250,000 visitors.

Once again requiring expansion because of the swelling collection in 1977, the museum was extended into the neighbouring former school of dentistry. After funding from the Heritage Lottery Fund as well as from the European Regional Development Fund, the University of Manchester and other sponsors, the museum was able to go through with a £12.5 million refurbishment, which was completed in 2003.

As aforementioned, the Manchester Museum now boasts an outstanding variety of different collections, each unique and inspiring in their own way. The most renowned of these concerns Egyptology – an extensive collection that includes objects dating from prehistoric Egypt (c. 10,000 BC) all the way up to the Byzantine era of around AD 600. As well as this, there is a 'Vivarium', an award-winning exhibition featuring live animals including frogs, amphibians and other reptiles, allowing visitors to

experience the thrill of a first-hand encounter with some of the rarest creatures on the planet.

The Manchester Museum also gained attention when 'Stan', a full-size skeletal replica of a Tyrannosaurus Rex, was introduced to the museum in 2004. The original skeleton was excavated in 1992 by the Black Hills Institute, located in South Dakota. It was named 'Stan' after Stan Sacrison, the palaeontologist who discovered the original skeleton. The original bones excavated were aged between 65-70 million years old and 70% of the original dinosaurs bones were found, making Stan the most complete T-rex ever discovered. The museum's replica of each of the 199 bones was produced with the use of silicone rubber moulds, into which polymer was then poured. The skeleton is now mounted on a large steel framework, fully displaying its majestic nature. The winner of the prestigious Lever Prize in 2015, the museum is perfect for those looking for an excursion that features a variety of historic attractions. From natural science to ancient history, there is something for everyone on offer at the Manchester Museum.

TRAFFORD CENTRE

The Trafford Centre is the second largest shopping centre in the UK, situated close to Trafford Park and about 5 miles from Manchester city centre. The centre opened in 1998 and was bought by Intu Properties in 2011 for £1.65 billion, the largest property acquisition in British history, and it currently has a staggering market value of £1.9 billion. A vibrant hub of leisure, entertainment and events, this famous local complex is renowned for its distinctive late-baroque granite and marble architecture, as well as the huge range of attractions it offers.

The site of the Trafford Centre was originally owned by the Manchester Ship Canal Company, until it was acquired in 1986 by Peel Holdings. An extensive planning process, one of the longest in the UK's history, was completed with the aim of building an out-of-town shopping centre on the site. Concerns included the effects that it might have on local retailers as well as potential traffic problems but it was ultimately passed by the House of Lords. Very good transport links and the huge numbers of shoppers the centre attracts to the area as a whole have since helped to alleviate such concerns.

With over 200 stores selling wares ranging from designer fashion to quality local products and with 10% of the UK's population living within a 45-minute drive of the centre, the Trafford Centre is a popular must-visit destination for any tourist. The Orient, the largest food court in Europe, combines an industrial Manchester 'steam ship' theme with designs from cultures around the world in spectacular fashion. The complex also boasts an opulent Great Hall, state-of-the-art entertainment venues including the UK's busiest cinema and numerous sports facilities located right next to the centre.

The shopping facilities are divided into a number

of different areas, each offering an enjoyable experience with their own distinct style. Peel Avenue is home to numerous high-street shops including H&M, Boots and the Apple Store, and is directly linked to the food court. Spacious, modern surroundings contrast with the classic architecture that gives the Trafford Centre its unique character and style. With two major department stores (Marks & Spencer and John Lewis) and an entrance via the first Selfridges outside London leading into its domed centre, the Avenue truly exemplifies some of the best of British brands.

Many high-end lifestyle, designer and fashion stores are located in the adjacent Regent Crescent, such as Victoria's Secret, Debenhams and BHS. Barton Square, a newer development in the Trafford Centre which opened in 2008, is connected to the main centre via a footbridge and is home to numerous family events including children's rides

and an annual Christmas market. The square's majestic outdoor architecture based around an Italian square is complemented by its magnificent fountains and statues, making it a 'hidden gem' well worth seeing.

There are also numerous plans for the future of the Trafford Centre. These include constructing a roof over Barton Square and expanding the flagship John Lewis and Marks and Spencer outlets. As well as this, long-term plans include expanding overall retail space by building retail areas on unused land, and attracting even more famous retailers who currently lack a presence such as House of Fraser or Primark. Planning applications have already been made for the expansion of the centre in the foreseeable future. The fact that the centre has amazing facilities and is constantly growing makes the Trafford Centre one of the best leisure complexes to visit in Europe.

The Great Hall & The Orient

The Orient is Europe's largest food court, with over 30 restaurants, cafés and bars ranging from fast food outlets to exquisite cuisine in a circular layout surrounding seating for 1,600 people. Restaurants range from TGI Friday's, Café Rouge and Nando's to Subway, Pizza Hut and the famous British fish-and-chips chain Harry Ramsden's. Fusing international designs from America, Italy, China, Egypt and Morocco with an architectural structure based around the industrial history of Manchester, its majestic surroundings combine rich local culture with historic international ties and influences. The ceiling is painted as a vast, heavenly sky, as if to open up the magnificent scen to the heavens and beyond. The Great Hall, whic opened in March 2007, houses five restauran and cafés in opulent surroundings, including a elegant sweeping staircase with hundreds of metr of Chinese marble and the largest chandelier in th world.

Odeon Cinema

The Odeon is a large 20-screen multiplex cinema, the busiest in the UK with an average of over 28,500 visitors per week. The cinema shows all of the latest films releases on many occasions throughout the day, with reasonable prices and high quality facilities. It features a state-of-the-art IMAX auditorium, combining powerful digital sound with a much larger, curved screen and elevating the movie-going experience by displaying films in crystal clear high definition. Tickets can be bought either from the cinema desks or via newly installe ticket machines, making use of modern technolog to streamline the movie-going experience. Wit retro arcade gaming machines and a wide selectio of snacks and treats, The Odeon arguably ranl among the best cinemas nationwide in terms of th outstanding entertainment experience it offers.

Laser Quest

The Trafford Centre also has its very own Laser Quest arena, providing an action-packed leisure attraction for visitors. With a large maze-like format, ramps and walkways concealed by swirling fog and dramatic lighting effects, the arena itself is specially designed to provide a unique and exciting gaming experience. The conventional format often consists of two teams of players wearing ponchos and attempting to tag each other to disable their opponents and earn points, with bonus points awarded for increased accuracy. Outside the arena, the centre has a simulated climbing wall known as 'The Rock', with varying speeds and inclines challenging players to stay on the wall for as long as possible. Laser Quest also has its own restaurant right next to the arena; although as the centre is situated a mere two-minute walk from The Orient food court, visitors are definitely not stuck for choice!

Paradise Island

A miniature golf attraction with a twist, Paradise Island Adventure Golf is located within The Orient and features two 18-hole indoor golf courses set among tropical surroundings. The 'Tiki Hut Trail' and 'Temple Ruins Adventure' courses offer challenging gameplay amidst vibrant wildlife, mystical stone carvings and exotic huts. With multiple levels and vouchers available when purchasing tickets at the Odeon to 'buy-one-game-get-one-free', the golf course is popular with many shoppers and visitors to the centre. Varying difficulty provided by a range of obstacles at each part of the course, as well as helpful facilities such as lockers, make this attraction both fun and customer-friendly. Sloping greens and diverse terrain make for a high quality leisure experience with a competitive side, providing yet another opportunity for a fun day out at the Trafford Centre.

Chill Factore

The UK's longest indoor ski slope and real snow centre, Chill Factore offers a huge range of snow-filled activities on its premier facilities. A massive 180m ski slope is complemented by a beginner's slope, luge track, sledging, tubing and snowboarding areas. Instructors hold sessions for anyone who wants to learn the ropes, with freestyle and racing events available for skilled enthusiasts. Initial lessons often cover slope etiquette, how to move around on skis and how to move up and down the slope, with further lessons providing a gre opportunity to learn skilled techniques. Special equipment such as skis and snowboards as well boots, gloves and helmets are all available. A them 'Alpine Village' area with shops, restaurants a bars offers panoramic viewing of the slopes, wi extras including high quality conference faciliti a 'snowplay' zone and even a 12m-high climbi wall.

Jump Nation

Jump Nation is the largest indoor trampoline area in the world, with a staggering 139 trampolines interconnected across the vast floor and walls of a giant sports hall. Inspired by popular trampoline parks in America and looking to exploit this gap in the UK market, the centre opened in August 2014. Hosting parties, team building events and family days out, the trampoline park can be used by up to 99 people at the same time. Fitness sessions and trampolining classes are also held on a regular basis, with professional, world-record breakir trampolinists using the centre on a regular basis. large foam pit allows users to practice crazy tric with an even softer landing, and an 'urban caf offers a variety of snacks and refreshments for break from the action. An enjoyable way of keepir fit and healthy, Jump Nation should appeal to tho who want to get active and have fun.

Soccerdome

Formerly the 'JJB Soccer Dome', this state-of-the-art indoor sports facility is the largest 5-a-side football centre in the world. Featuring dedicated local leagues, 19 high all-purpose indoor pitches and 4 floodlit outdoor pitches, the centre is a hub for aspiring young players of the game. Qualified coaches and specialised sessions are held on a daily basis using high quality football equipment and facilities, along with regular fixtures and tournaments. Local and national level leagues also means there is a competitive aspect for teams of young people, with scouts for football teams sometimes present. The centre also includes a brand new multisport arena, with a state-of-the-art surface available for badminton, basketball, dodgeball and netball games. A licensed bar situated close to the pitches provides a place to take a break and rehydrate, and dedicated function rooms can be booked as part of children's parties and other events.

Airkix

Located in the heart of Trafford's Leisure Village, Airkix Indoor Skydiving offers an exhilarating and challenging experience. An indoor wind tunnels simulates the airflows of free fall, in a safe environment protected from the various weather risks of outdoor skydiving. Highly qualified and experienced instructors guide first-time fliers through the basics and provide demonstrations of more advanced skydiving techniques, as well as supervising more advanced skydivers who use the centre as a high quality training facility. Professional equipment is used, with the safety of users a priority which is always taken into account. A seating area provides a direct view of the action, with an Italian café offerings authentic cuisine for visitors. With numerous transport links by rail and bus, Airkix is a unique sports attraction for anyone with a taste for extreme sports or just brave enough to try it!

Event City

Event City is one of the largest exhibition centres outside London, situated on a privately owned 24-acre site next to the industrial Trafford Park area. The building was initially built in 1995 as a factory for Manchester Tobacco, and went on to be leased to Argos for use as a warehouse, as well as becoming the 'Museum of Museums' for just over a year. Subsequently converted to its current use in 2011, this modern and sophisticated centre provides planning, operational and catering services for a variety of events. This includes having hosted The X Factor auditions for the Manchester area, the Commonwealth Heavyweight Boxing Title and annual premiere Christmas parties which attract over 10,000 visitors. With bookings beyond 2021 already confirmed, the highly popular centre regularly hosts numerous consumer, hobby and trade shows, as well as being available as an exquisite choice of venue for private functions.

Sea Life

Over 5,000 sea creatures and 30 display tanks make Sea Life Manchester an exciting aquatic experience. Fascinating talks and interactive experiences, including a hands-on activity with crabs and starfish, are complemented by fun children's booklets which can be used to collect stamps from each area of the aquarium. An 'ocean tunnel' through a large tank provides a close-up view of life under the sea, with shoals of fish and a giant sea turtle gliding next to and above visitors. Recent additions to the aquarium include octopuses, known for their intelligence with the famous Paul the Octopus who made many accurate predictions in the 2010 World Cup having been housed at a Sea Life centre in Germany. Sea Life Manchester also offers a 'Sea Trek', a unique experience providing the opportunity to walk at the bottom of a large fish tank in a diving helmet surrounded by powerful sharks and a giant sea turtle.

SPORTSCITY

Previously derelict land in the deprived area of Beswick, East Manchester, 2002's Commonwealth Games catalysed the development of the area, now home to a huge variety of state-of-the-art sports facilities, as well as the spectacular Etihad Stadium boasting a capacity in excess of 55,000. Located within the Medlock Valley and a mere two miles from the city centre, Sportscity has the highest concentration of sporting venues in Europe, making it a hub of sporting excellence.

Developed for the hugely successful 2002 Commonwealth Games, Sportscity is now home to Manchester City Football Club. Owned by the extremely wealthy Sheikh Mansour, Manchester City are rapidly evolving into one of the best teams in the world, and the sheer beauty of the Etihad Stadium is an apt stage for the mesmerising football their world stars play. In addition to this centrepiece of Sportscity, the National Cycling Centre, consisting of the Manchester Velodrome and the state-of-the-art National Indoor BMX Arena, offers unparalleled professional cycling facilities. Furthermore, Sportscity is home to the National Squash Centre and Regional Arena for Athletics. The recent addition of Manchester City's £50 million training and leisure complex has further bolstered Sportscity's enthralling array of assets.

The stunning venues that Sportscity has developed provide phenomenal facilities for elite athletes, in unison with an enriched community development programme in an attempt to nurture the stars of tomorrow towards the pinnacle of their sports careers. Numerous other projects and additions to Sportscity have been rejected to protect the stellar quality and refined character of the complex; for example, at a mere two miles from the city centre, Sportscity was the proposed location for the UK's first 'super casino', but the plan was rejected at the last minute by the House of Lords. In addition to this, Sportscity was the site of a proposed 85m wind turbine. However, fundamental safety issues led to this proposal also being abandoned.

Beswick was once a forlorn and despondent image of misery and despair. However, in a dramatic turn of events that was driven by the iconic 2002 Commonwealth Games, this image has been transformed into one of accomplishment and prosperity in the form of Sportscity. The area has become the heart of sporting excellence in Great Britain.

Etihad Stadium

The City of Manchester Stadium, popularly known as the Etihad Stadium due to sponsorship by Etihad Airways, was designed as part of Manchester's unsuccessful bid for the 2000 Summer Olympics. It was built as the centrepiece of Sportscity, the home of the 2002 Commonwealth Games, at a cost of £110 million. After the games, it was converted into a football stadium and became the home of Manchester City Football Club, who moved there from Maine Road in 2003 after signing a 250-year lease. Originally with two levels around the entire ground and a third tier on two sides of the ground, the post-conversion capacity was 47,800. However, in March 2010, Manchester City agreed to allow redevelopment of land surrounding the stadium by the city council, including an expansion of the stadium to boost the capacity to 60,000.

Originally, plans to build a stadium in east Manchester were made in 1990 as part of the city's bid for the 2000 Summer Olympics, with the council funding a design of an 80,000 seater stadium. However, following Manchester's successful bid for the 2002 Commonwealth Games, the plans were used from the Olympic bid. The stadium cost a staggering £110 million to build of which £77 million was paid by Sport England, the remainder being funded by Manchester City Council. The first event hosted at the ground was the Commonwealth Games Opening Ceremony attended by Her Majesty The Queen, among other notable public figures. Throughout ten days of fierce competition, the stadium was home to all athletics events as well as the rugby sevens fixtures. During the exceptionally successful games, four Commonwealth Records were set at the stadium, including a new record for the women's triple jump.

Following the Commonwealth Games, the multi-purpose stadium was converted into a dedicated football venue. Such was the incredibly successful nature of the games on an athletic level that this decision drew widespread criticism throughout the athletics world, with iconic figures such as Sebastian Coe condemning the decision. Despite this, redevelopment plans were carried out with great success and as a result, sections of the athletics track were transferred to other athletics stadiums and the ground level was lowered to make way for another level of seating. The work spanned an entire, arduous year and added 12,000 seats at a colossal cost of £30 million, which was paid by Manchester City F.C. who made it their home at the start of the 2003-04 season.

The first goal at the stadium was part of a 2-1 victory for Manchester City against the might of the Spanish giants F.C. Barcelona on August 10th 2003, with Nicolas Anelka scoring 38 minutes into the match. In addition to being home of Manchester City Football Club, the stadium has also hosted several other esteemed sporting events, becoming the 50th English stadium to host an international football match when England played Japan in 2004. It has also hosted countless rugby league fixtures, including that of England vs. Australia in the Tri-Nations series of 2004. Furthermore, in 2008, the stadium hosted the enthralling UEFA Cup Final between Rangers and Zenit St. Petersburg.

The Etihad Stadium is still owned by Manchester City Council, continuing to be leased to Manchester City Football Club. Following the headline 20(takeover of Manchester City which made it t) richest club in the world, rumour had it that t) club was considering about buying the stadiu from the council, although this ultimately didr happen.

Outside of the football season, the stadium hos numerous concerts and is one of the UK's large music venues. It has a maximum capacity of 60,0(for performances, with some of the most outstandir artists in the music industry performing ther including the Red Hot Chilli Peppers, Take Th and U2. Unfortunately, summer activities such concerts and boxing matches typically reduce t) quality of the pitch. Rather comically, at the start the 2008 season the pitch was of insufficient qual and as a result, Manchester City were forced to pl their first UEFA Cup qualifying match at the mu smaller Oakwell Stadium, the home ground lower-league Barnsley F.C..

Manchester Regional Arena

Fashioned as a less-than-glamorous warm up track for the 2002 Commonwealth Games, in recent years, Manchester Regional Arena has hosted more notable events, including the AAA Championships and the Paralympics World Cup. In addition to this, it was home to Manchester City Women's Football Club until their move to the adjacent Etihad Campus in 2014. The outdoor arena consists of an 8-lane 400m running track around the perimeter of the central field, as well as having a capacity of up to 6,500 which is commendable for a relatively small, local stadium. The indoor area also consists of a 4-lane 200m running track, a 6-lane 60m sprint track and an indoor jumping pit.

Philips Park

Picturesque, tranquil and serene, Philips Park offers a peaceful getaway at the heart of the city. Opened on 22nd August 1846, the park consists of 31 acres of green land surrounding the Sportscity complex. The principal intention of the park was to act as a catalyst for encouraging healthier lifestyles for the residents of Manchester, providing the area for a large array of outdoor classes soon after its opening. Entry to the park is free to the public and offers an incredible display of stunning natural beauty, seldom available in the vastly industrialised city of Manchester.

The park is a mosaic of woodland, grassland, hills and water, and has its own unique orchard which acts a show-field for events. As well as this, there is a picnic area and a large pond with a dipping area, allowing visitors to cool off in Manchester's warm summer months... or, perhaps more accurately, serving as a public ice bath all year round! There are also several recreational facilities available at the park, such as a ball court, junior football pitch, a bowling green and a pavilion. The park effectively caters to the diverse demographic of inner-city Manchester.

The secret to Philips Park's success is its maintenance by a well-organised and close-knit friends group, allowing for a stimulating and comforting atmosphere in the park. A rarity for a city centre park, the group works tirelessly to organise events, educational visits and health walks to benefit the public when they visit the park. The park has been a prominent venue for a multitude of events in the local area, such as the 'Party in the Park' which truly captures the warm essence of the local community. It also serves as the host for local 'Bonfire Night' celebrations, with a sensational fireworks display held each year.

The awarding of the reputable 'Green Flag' status to the park by the Civic Trust in 2005 is symbolic of the lush greenery and incomprehensible beauty that makes up the park. Easily accessible by car, bus, cycle and foot, Philips Park serves as the ideal location for a memorable day out, ideal for enjoying the typically sunnier weather of the warm summer months.

The Velodrome

When built in 1994, Manchester Velodrome, part of the National Cycling Centre, was Britain's first indoor cycling track. It has since been an intrinsic part of the exponential growth and astounding international success that British cycling has enjoyed over the past two decades. The National Cycling Centre was funded by the government and the Foundation for Sport and Art. Construction of the Velodrome itself began in the early 1990s. Since completion in 1994, it has hosted countless illustrious events in the cycling calendar, including the Commonwealth Games once (2002) and the UCI Track Cycling World Championships on three occasions (1996, 2000 and 2008).

As of March 2008, the National Cycling Centre had been the site of over fifteen world-record rides, including the 4000m team pursuit world record set by the Great British men's team at the 2008 World Championships. The velodrome is widely considered to be one of the finest professional tracks in the world by cycling's very best, at 250 metres in length and with the banking at a 42 degree incline to the centre of the racetrack. The track has been ridden on at high-octane, exhilarating speeds by the best cyclists in the sport, including the eleven-time world champion and six-time Olympic champion Sir Chris Hoy and Victoria Pendleton MBE, the winner of nine world titles including a record six titles in the individual sprint competition alone.

To further consolidate Manchester's status as the centre of cycling in Britain, the state-of-the-art National Indoor BMX Arena opened in Augu 2011, housing the UK's only permanent indoc BMX track adjacent to the Velodrome. Howeve the many opportunities for cycling in Mancheste do not end there, with the 12km Clayton Vale trac on the doorstep of the Velodrome. In addition this, the Manchester Velodrome is also the fir facility to offer tracks developed for accessible bik used by disabled riders, with each of four differer such trails graded to suit different abilities. Th Velodrome truly is a wonderful facility tha encourages participation by all.

Not only does the Manchester Velodrome offer multitude of stunning cycling facilities, but it als offers other high quality sports facilities too. Wit ten badminton courts, two basketball courts and tw futsal/korfball courts, the National Cycling Centr is also a focal point for sports in Manchester as whole. The Mancunian population has relished th opportunity and participation in sport has thrive as a result, with public sessions at the centre ofte fully booked many weeks in advance,

Open seven days a week, Manchester Velodrom is easily accessible with regular bus services and Metrolink service running directly from centra Manchester to the complex. Furthermore, th Velodrome offers the unique opportunity allowing you to take your own bicycle onto th track, providing it meets the necessary specification which are detailed on the National Cycling Centre' website.

THE QUAYS

Also known as Salford Quays to local residents, The Quays was previously the site of the larger section of Manchester Docks, first opened in 1894 by Queen Victoria. At their height, the docks were the third busiest in Britain. However, in the 1970s, limits on ship sizes and containerisation meant that the docks declined. After the closure of the dockyards in 1982, the area became one of the UK's largest and most ambitious urban regeneration projects. Salford City Council acquired parts of the docks within a year, and began redevelopment in 1985, building dams to isolate the docks and to clear water pollution. An internal waterway network, roads and bridges were created, along with a promenade along the waterfront.

Soon, public and private funding led to hotels, cinemas, offices and housing all being built in the area. A number of landmark attractions, including The Lowry and Imperial War Museum North, received planning permission and were built during the late 1990s and early 2000s. More recently, the flagship Media City UK was constructed in The

Quays, boosting its status as an exceptional urban development even further. Thousands of jobs and hundreds of businesses have moved to the area, making it a vibrant urban centre built out of the historic docks of the Manchester Ship Canal.

A huge array of sports, businesses and residential buildings are located in The Quays. The site of the Great Manchester Swim, the area is well-known for its state-of-the-art watersports facilities. In addition, the area is extremely well connected with direct links to Manchester city centre via a dedicated Metrolink tram line opened in 1999. Easily accessible bus and road links also ensure that the area is often bustling with tourists and visitors from across the UK and the world. A hub of famous attractions and exciting events, The Quays is most definitely an area of Manchester worth visiting.

MediaCity UK

A 200-acre site on the banks of Manchester Ship Canal, Media City UK is home to a whole host of different educational and media-related firms, including multiple BBC and ITV studios and a University of Salford campus. Created as part of large-scale decentralisation from London and opening in stages from 2007 onwards, Media City UK is twice the size of London's Trafalgar Square. The development's outdoor spaces which include a piazza have numerous bars, cafés and restaurants, and attract high levels of footfall during both the day and night.

The BBC, Media City's principal tenant, has moved a whole host of channels and programmes to the development including Match of The Day, Blue Peter, BBC Sport, Radio 5 Live and the BBC Philharmonic Orchestra among others. Tours of the behind-the-scenes action are available, with visits to music and news studios as well as the sets of popular programmes offering a unique experience of what goes on in the making of many famous BBC productions. An interactive CBBC tour for kids with the opportunity to meet the stars of children's programmes is also available.

Numerous events are held throughout the year at Media City UK. Two large public outdoor spaces provide a spacious outdoor location, and the spectacular waterfront piazza can accommodate up to 5,000 people for larger-scale events. Equipped with a double-sided big screen, this dynamic venue has hosted a large variety of high-profile events in the past, including the Gok Wan Clothes Show Live and The Voice UK auditions in Manchester. There is also an Open Centre located at the front of the Studios building, which can hold up to 400 people in total and has hosted numerous conferences, media launches and fashion shows in the past. Providing modern indoor space with an impressive mezzanine level, this events facility comes with stunning views over the surrounding buildings and development.

ITV Granada moved to Media City UK in March 2013, and has since filmed the famous British soap Coronation Street in a nearby ITV studio. ITV completed the first phase of its move to the area in 2013, making the Orange Tower home to teams from CITV, Granada Reports and The Jeremy Kyle Show among others. The neighbouring 'Pie Factory' has also become a successful TB and commercial production site, with recent productions including The Street, The Royle Family's Christmas special and Paradox. As a result of the development, thousands of jobs and educational opportunities have been created in the area.

In 2011, Media City UK was awarded the status of the first sustainable community in the entire world. Among the innovative green energy projects, the

area has made use of its own power plant which provides for the buildings in a self-sufficient manner. Tram, bus and cycle routes have also been expanded, in order to reduce traffic congestion and keep the area more pollution-free. In addition, high quality technology services are based in Media City, with a data centre and on-demand computing available for businesses who wish to take advantage of more modern and advanced technologies.

Media City UK is well-connected, boasting a 2,200 space car park installed in 2011 and a tram stop specially built to make the development more accessible. With 70,000 square feet worth of offices, 250,000 feet of HD studios, 378 high-quality apartments and 220 Holiday Inn rooms, the development is truly extraordinary in terms of what it has brought to the local community. A public park and events space offer a multitude of attractions for visitors, alongside shops such as a WHSmith and a number of well-known local restaurants. Media City has something to offer for everyone, and is an example of how re-development has helped to make Manchester a vibrant hub for both business and tourism.

Imperial War Museum

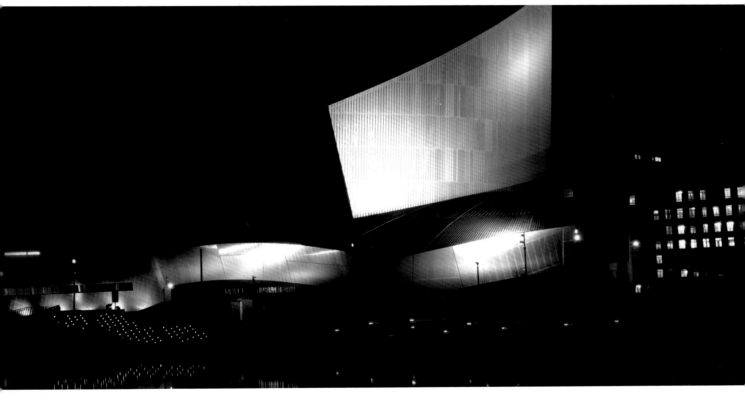

The Imperial War Museum North is located in The Quays and is 1 of 5 such museums in the country, with many state-of-the-art exhibitions within the museum. The Quays was heavily blitzed during the Second World War, and so the museum has a significant focus upon the impacts of the 'blitzkrieg' bombing campaign on industrial Manchester. The building is aluminium-clad, designed to disorientate visitors to reflect the chaotic nature of war. Unsurprisingly, the museum won the Building Award in the 2003 British Construction Industry Awards, as well as having been shortlisted for the 2004 Stirling Prize.

Occupying a site overlooking the Manchester Ship Canal in Trafford Park, the museum is the first branch of the Imperial War Museum to be located in the North of England, and aims to explore the impact of modern conflicts on people in society. The museum consists of a chronological display encircling the perimeter of the main gallery space, with the floor curving away from a nominal 'North Pole' situated near the gallery's entrance. Imitating the curvature of the Earth and signifying the international facet of Manchester's wartime history, this gallery provides an exciting window into history. There are also multiple, smaller galleries situated throughout the building.

The museum was an instant success, with 470,000

visitors in its first year of operation. Its eye-catching, award-winning architecture and huge variety of exhibitions, such as "Mixing It - the changing faces of wartime Britain", make the museum a highly interesting and original place to visit. Audio and visual presentations are projected into the main gallery space on an hourly basis, involving visitors in an immersive educational experience. Permanent exhibitions include "The Picture Show", which makes use of a surround sound system and digital imagery projected onto a 30-feet high wall to create a realistic visual experience of wartime Britain.

The main gallery of the museum consists of a display of wartime memorabilia along a 200m-long hall, including a Russian T-34 tank, a US Harrier jet and the 13-pounder field gun which fired the British Army's very first shot of the First World War. There are also various artefacts of more modern warfare which the Imperial War Museum is famous for. A vehicle captured by British Army Engineers during the opening stages of the Iraq War in 2003 may be found at the museum, with an ex-Iraqi Army T-55 tank having been on display outside the museum since August 2008.

Since opening in July 2002, the Imperial War Museum North has run a successful volunte[e] programme in partnership with the Manchest[er] Museum. Financed by the Department for Cultu[re] Media and Sport as part of a national museu[m] it also relies upon self-generated income, y[et] admission remains free for all those who wish [to] visit. This fantastic centre of Manchester's ri[ch] history and culture supports educational goa[ls] seeking to engage local people who risk soc[ial] exclusion and bring them into the heritage of t[he] area. Such projects mean that the museum n[ot] only contributes to the local area in a historica[lly] significant way, but also socially as an importa[nt] part of the local community.

This fantastic tourist destination also featur[es] specially planned family-friendly days durin[g] the holidays, held in the learning studios of t[he] museum. These days make use of themes relate[d] to the World Wars as part of popular culture, su[ch] as the well-known children's history book seri[es] "Horrible Histories" and the classic BBC televisi[on] sitcom "Dad's Army". For anyone with a passion f[or] history or simply interested in learning about t[he] wars of the past, this museum is both fascinati[ng] and eye-opening!`

Old Trafford

Old Trafford is the home of Manchester United, the world-famous and internationally successful football club. Also known as the Theatre of Dreams, it has a huge capacity of 76,365, making it the largest football stadium in the country. It has been the home ground of Manchester United ever since 1910, although the club was once forced to share a ground with local rivals Manchester City at Maine Road due to the extensive damage that the bombs of the Second World War did to Old Trafford.

6 February 1958, the day of the Munich air disaster, was a tragic date for Manchester United and shocked the world of football. The football team was returning from a European Cup match against Red Star Belgrade, when the flight stopped to refuel in Munich. After abandoning take-off from Munich twice, the captain decided to attempt take-

off for a third time, by which time snow was falling and a layer of slush had formed on the runway. The aircraft skidded through the slush and destroyed a fence, tearing of the left wing before hitting a house. The British Airways plane caught fire with 38 passengers and 6 crew on board. Seven of the Manchester United players, known as the 'Busby Babes' at the time, were among the 21 that died, with the victims also including sports journalists and club officials.

Today, 4 all-seater stands make up the Theatre of Dreams. The largest of them is the North Stand, which can hold up to 26,000 spectators, and which was renamed The Sir Alex Ferguson Stand in tribute to the man regarded by many as the greatest manager of all time. He won a total of 49 trophies for Manchester United, including 13 Premier

League titles, 10 community shields, 5 FA Cups, 4 League Cups, 2 Champions League trophies, 1 Club World Cup, and 1 Super Cup. Sir Alex famously led Manchester United to win the historic 'treble' in the 1998-1999 season, winning the Champions League with 2 goals in three minutes of added time in Barcelona. In November 2012, a statue of Sir Alex Ferguson was unveiled, standing at an impressive 9 feet tall.

Old Trafford offers the unique opportunity to go behind the scenes at the stadium with a stadium tour, allowing everyone to see the ground through the perspective of the Manchester United legends themselves. The 80-minute tours allow you to go the changing rooms and walk through the player tunnel, following the footsteps of the United grea The museum showcases the historical achievemen and many trophies that Manchester United hav won over the years, with rare memorabilia an interactive exhibitions, enabling you to learn mor about the biggest club in the world. Howeve nothing beats actually experiencing the atmospher of a football match at Old Trafford.

Emirates Old Trafford

Emirates Old Trafford is the home of Lancashire County Cricket Club, the famous cricket club of one of England's 18 major counties. It can host up to 27,000 fans and is one of the largest cricket grounds in the country. It is England's second oldest test venue and arguably one of the most renowned, featuring as the venue for the first ever Ashes test held in England in July 1884, and as the location for two Cricket World Cup semi-finals. In an effort to safeguard international cricket at the venue, extensive redevelopment of the ground began in 2009, in order to increase its capacity and modernise its high quality facilities.

During World War II, Old Trafford cricket ground was used as a transit camp for soldiers returning from Dunkirk. Similarly to Manchester United's Old Trafford, the cricket ground was also struck by heavy bombing, destroying numerous stands. Despite the extensive damage, cricket resumed almost as soon as the war finished, with nothing deterring the 76,856 fans who attended to spectate England beating Australia over three days in the first match after the war.

There have been a number of historically significant cricketing moments which have taken place at Old Trafford. In 1981, Sir Ian Bothan scored 118 runs, including 6 sixes, which is the second greatest total in an Ashes innings. In 1990, Sachin Tendulkar scored his first test century at the grounds when just 17 years old, making him the second youngest 'centurion' ever - he went on to become what many regard as the greatest batsman the game has ever seen.

Emirates Old Trafford has many facilities located within the stadium, including The Point, which is a 1,200 seater conference centre. The Pavilion is also a versatile venue for conferences, meetings and events, accommodating up to 700 guests across 8 suites, with a footbridge linking The Point to The Pavilion. Lots of events, corporate workshops, training and meetings also take place in the state-of-the-art AJ Bell Players & Media Centre. The Indoor Cricket Centre is also located within the Old Trafford grounds, with 5 indoor nets used by cricketers of all ages and abilities.

ABOUT US

urbanMCR is a company made up of a group of students from Altrincham Grammar School for Boys, near Manchester. The company was formed in October 2015 through the Young Enterprise Company programme, a national competition held at schools throughout the country.

Having been inspired by the community around us, we wanted to share our passion for Manchester, and all it has to offer, with the rest of the world. So we decided to create Manchester Discovered.

Manchester Discovered features the most interesting and unique places to visit on a day out in Manchester, in an attempt to show the world what a wonderful place we are proud to live in.

Every single photograph on the pages of this book has been taken by ourselves, with our team of dedicated writers and graphic designers having worked tirelessly to produce its unique and outstanding content.

During the production of this book, we've tried [to] share our own niche knowledge of this special [city] as well as learning a few things ourselves along [the] way via our thorough use of online, literary a[nd] on-the-ground research sources. And after m[any] painstaking hours of hard work, we're proud [of] what we've managed to achieve.

Thank you for purchasing our book and support[ing] our local enterprise, and we hope you've enjo[yed] your journey through the pages of Manchester w[ith] us!